BLACK BELT® BOOKS

MW01008140

SILAT
FOR THE STREET

Using the Ancient Martial Art for Self-Defense in the 21st Century

Burton Richardson

BLACK BELT BOOKS

SILAT
FOR THE STREET

Using the Ancient Martial Art for Self-Defense in the 21st Century

Burton Richardson

Special Projects Editor: Vicki Baker
Copy Chief: Jeannine Santiago
Photography: Robert Reiff
Graphic Design: John Bodine
Vintage Photos: Burton Richardson

Printed in the United States of America
Library of Congress Control Number: 2016933706

ISBN-13: 978-0-89750-212-2

First Printing 2016

Warning
This book is presented only as a means of preserving a unique aspect of the heritage of the martial arts. Neither the publisher nor the author makes any representation, warranty or guarantee that the techniques described or illustrated in this book will be safe or effective in any self-defense situation or otherwise. You may be injured if you apply or train in the techniques illustrated in this book and neither the publisher nor the author is responsible for any such injury that may result. It is essential that you consult a physician regarding whether or not to attempt any technique described in this book. Specific self-defense responses illustrated in this book may not be justified in any particular situation in view of all of the circumstances or under applicable federal, state or local law. Neither the publisher nor the author makes any representation or warranty regarding the legality or appropriateness of any technique mentioned in this book.

BLACK BELT BOOKS
A Division of OHARA PUBLICATIONS, INC.
World Leader in Martial Arts Publications

ABOUT THE AUTHOR

Burton Richardson is one of the most sought-after functional-self-defense instructors in the world. Each year he tours the globe, giving seminars and private lessons to martial arts instructors, students, military and law-enforcement personnel.

Richardson grew up in Carson, California. As a boy, he spent a lot of time after school at Scott Park, a place that would have a major impact on his future life. This is where, as a youngster, he first experienced a shooting, peeked in awe at a gym full of *karateka* and was shown a magazine about Bruce Lee. It was much later that Richardson learned that his childhood hero Kato, of *The Green Hornet* TV series, was played by Bruce Lee.

Richardson first went to the Filipino Kali/Jun Fan Academy, which was about a mile from his house, in 1979. He began studying directly with *guro/sifu* Dan Inosanto and guro/sifu Richard Bustillo in 1980. That year, Richardson also started at the University of Southern California, studying biology and tackling a four-year writing and literature honors program called Thematic Option while playing on the baseball team.

With college behind him, Richardson took a year off from his intense studies before going to medical school. He decided that during that year, he would eschew outside pressures and, for the first time in his life, do exactly what he wanted to do — train at the Inosanto Academy. Living in a tiny camper trailer in the parking lot of a dog and cat hospital near downtown Los Angeles, Richardson dedicated himself to martial arts. That one-year sabbatical from school turned into a lifetime study of the fighting arts. It took him five years to get out of that miserable trailer where he heard gunfire every night, witnessed a drive-by shooting across the street and routinely picked up stray bullets in the parking lot.

Through dedication to training and consistency, Richardson earned high-level instructor status from many luminaries of the arts. Years of intense training under Dan Inosanto led to full instructor's credentials in Filipino *kali* and in Bruce Lee's *jeet kune do* and *Jun Fan gung fu* concepts. Richardson became a senior full instructor under the late JKD great sifu Larry Hartsell. Master Chai Sirisute awarded Richardson's Thai boxing instructorship, while the title of "guro" was achieved in Indonesian *pencak silat* under the guidance of *pendekar* Paul de Thouars. Richardson earned his instructorship in *kali ilustrisimo* in Manila under grandmaster Antonio Ilustrisimo, master Tony Diego and master Christopher Ricketts. Richardson is also one of the original Dog Brothers, given the nickname Lucky Dog in the 1980s.

Richardson earned his black belt in Brazilian *jiu-jitsu* under multiple-time BJJ and mixed-martial arts world champion Egan Inoue. The author also cornered world champion Baret Yoshida in several Abu Dhabi Combat Club Submission Wrestling World Championships. Richardson was training and coaching since the inception of no-holds barred fighting, which later became MMA. He coached and cornered MMA fighters the world over, most notably Enson Inoue, Egan Inoue and Chris Leben. Richardson has even journeyed to South Africa several times to train with Zulu warriors in their method of stick fighting. In 2014, he earned his instructor credential in *krav maga* from Israeli special-forces instructor Nir Maman.

Richardson is known for his ability to break down and explain the functional aspects of martial arts for better understanding and more efficient training. Richardson's primary goal is to provide the most functional techniques, tactics and training methods for realistic self-defense. He puts all his years in the sciences to good use, using the scientific method to properly test techniques before he teaches them. He takes the time to highlight the fine details that often make the difference between success and failure, both in the art and in life.

Richardson hopes that his students never have to use their art to defend themselves, but he prepares each and every one of them for that eventuality. He prefers focusing on functional fight preparation to teaching the artistic portion that could get someone killed in a street encounter. "Training people to actually fight is much more difficult on the body and the ego," he says, "but the lessons learned are real and can be used to build the character tools necessary to overcome obstacles in your life every single day. My ultimate goal is to develop great people who are physically and mentally strong enough to be kind to everyone they meet."

DEDICATION

First and foremost, I dedicate this book to Sarah. She is my wife, training partner, mother to our child and best friend. Never once has she tried to dissuade me from training, even when that meant traveling to distant places to attend seminars. Thank you for always having my back.

I also dedicate this book to my mentor *tuhon* Dan Inosanto. Thank you for always leading by example.

And I dedicate this book to martial artists everywhere who are on the path of constant improvement. I do hope you find my work useful for your quest toward martial and personal mastery.

CONTENTS

FOREWORD

It was an honor to be asked to write the foreword to Burton Richardson's *Silat for the Street.* I've known Burt for years, since we trained together at Dan Inosanto's Academy of Martial Arts when it was in Marina del Rey, California. In those pre-Dog Brothers days (mid-1980s), we had a Midnight Fight Club, which was primarily full-contact fighting sessions with sticks, knives and other weapons fighting that Danny was gracious enough to let us do after classes. "No killings tonight, turn the lights out and lock up when you're done. Have fun!" were his sage and easy-to-follow instructions. For the record, we were able to oblige most of the time. During these sessions, I first had a chance to get to know Burt as a fighter and then as a training partner and friend.

Even at that time, Burt was known as the *"pencak silat* guy," a style/system that I had had *some* exposure to (mostly as a theory) but not much in a real-contact scenario. So I was a little skeptical of its practical application when it came to fighting, especially in conjunction with weapons. That said, after watching and fighting with Burt over the course of several midnight sessions, it became clear to everyone there that 1) Burt was very game and willing to put his training to the test, dish out lumps, take his lumps and learn from both, and 2) pencak silat might actually work, even in a full-contact weapons context! What we found particularly effective was the way his sweeps seemed to come from nowhere whenever he closed the gap. He would land his opponents awkwardly on their hips or backside on the concrete floor (no padding in those days), which certainly increased everyone's awareness of just how effective a system can be when put through the process of real-time experience. Over time, everyone got better at their specialty — closing became cleaner, recognition became quicker and footwork, power, purpose and even our drills all evolved. And *that* was the point of those nights.

Burt tells you throughout the book that this does not happen overnight and that the techniques and moves aren't guaranteed to be successful the first time. Go in knowing that you will try and you will probably fail early on, but you must try. Understanding the technique follows your attempts to actually use it. And by "actually use it," I mean you need to practice on someone who is not cooperating. At that point, you will see the divide that is in most martial arts — fighting versus forms. The fighters will say that without real resistance, you're just kidding yourself and all you're do-

ing is a flowery ritualistic dance. The other side will claim that not everyone is cut out to fight, that you can simulate fighting through drills, and that they are preserving the art vis-à-vis *kata* (training exercises), *carenza* (solo practice) and *kembangan* (flower dance). Each side is right until they try to minimize or, worse, eliminate the importance of the other. In times of danger, the "martial" fighters prevail and much of the "art" is lost. In times of peace, the reverse occurs and much of the "martial" is removed or outlawed.

The correct — and most difficult — path is to honor both. How? It's simple and yet unexpectedly elusive: Keep it real, be honest with yourself and your training partners, and be aware that in order to evolve, you must be receptive to things that may be outside your training comfort zone. Trust me, nothing is more politically incorrect these days than the truth. Whether you are a student or instructor, there will be many attempts to lead you astray and get you to sugarcoat reality. Within your group, there will often be resistance to accepting facts or even exploring other methods of doing things. If you can resist this urge and continue to be curious about things outside the box, then you are on the right path. Fortunately, Burt explains the "street" side of a move, how to drill it and then some history as to how it came about or how he had an occasion to use it. He has had the opportunity to train with the best in the world, and in this book, he is sharing that opportunity with all of us. So in that spirit, "No killings tonight, turn the lights out and lock up when you're done. Have fun!"

— Eric "Top Dog" Knaus

PREFACE

My primary responsibility as a *silat* instructor is to teach my students how to fight. I assume that one or more of my students will someday get into a life-threatening situation, so my responsibility is to train each and every one for that eventuality. That is my primary reason for writing this book and why only pressure-tested fighting techniques and training methods that have proved their effectiveness are emphasized.

Drawing from my background as a scientist, I use an evidence-based approach. That means that I don't rely on theory or hypothesis but only on actual evidence derived from realistic, valid fighting tests. So I pledge that I will only teach techniques that I have used in fighting or sparring, or that I have seen others use in fighting or sparring. I am not saying that other methods don't work, but I won't teach them as functional until I have solid evidence of their efficacy.

I don't know everything, but I can assure you that everything in this book is useful for true combat if practiced as prescribed. I will also point out the errors in thinking and training that lead many away from functional fighting. We have to realize that knowledge is not power. The ability to apply your knowledge under pressure is true power. It isn't a question of whether a technique can possibly work. The real question is, "Can you actually make it work against someone who is fighting you 100 percent?" That is why you must engage in the functional training to functionalize your favorite techniques.

Please let me know whether you have found other ideas that have proved effective. I am always looking for a better way and sincerely welcome your input.

NOTES ON TERMINOLOGY

Pencak (or *pentjak*) *silat* is an Indonesian term, but in this book, it is used to describe the arts that originated in the ancient Majapahit empire. This kingdom spanned from the southern Philippines across Indonesia and up through what is now known as Malaysia, Thailand, Myanmar, Vietnam, Cambodia and Laos. The same Majapahit culture was pervasive through the entire area, from the food to clothing to music to dance and to the amazing fighting arts. There are many names and hundreds of individual styles, but for the purposes of this book, the umbrella term silat is used to cover all of them.

Also, English terms are used to describe the techniques and positions. Bear in mind that in Indonesia alone, there are more than 500 languages and dialects spoken, so to choose one particular language, even if it is the official language of Bahasa, would not be representative of the majority of Southeast Asian martial arts. Because the book is written in English, it is easiest to stick to English descriptions. Indonesian terminology is included for some moves that are commonly known by their native monikers.

ACKNOWLEDGMENTS

I want to extend my sincere, profound gratitude to every *silat* instructor who has helped me better understand my martial path. There are three men who generously provided me with the great majority of my training in the Southeast Asian arts.

First, and certainly foremost, is *tuhon* Dan Inosanto, my mentor in silat, *jeet kune do, kali, muay Thai* and life itself. He is the embodiment of what a martial artist should be. *Maraming salamat po* (thank you very much, with great respect).

To my second major silat instructor, the late *pak* Herman Suwanda. We spent a great deal of time together in and out of class. Always kind, Herman's knowledge base of many silat systems was incredibly vast, as was his skill in displaying these arts. *Terima kasih* (thank you) and I miss you.

And to my third major silat instructor, the late *pendekar* Paul de Thouars. As funny and charming as he was deadly, Paul passed on an incredibly precise application of pencak silat through the *serak* style and his own system of *bukti negara.* From levers to angles to the techniques themselves, Paul's methods amazed all who experienced them. I miss those days of hard training and harder laughing. *Hormat* (respects)!

I also have been able to train with many other silat instructors, some just on seminars and others for just a few private training sessions. They, too, have influenced me, and I appreciate their generosity. I don't want to make it sound like I was a full-time student because that would be disrespectful to those who spent years with them. But I would like to acknowledge the guidance and influence of a few who were especially impactful: pendekar Victor de Thouars of the serak system, grandmaster Willem de Thouars of *kuntao,* pendekar Jim Ingram of *mustika kwitang,* and an instructor from Southeast Asia who will read this but wishes not to be publicized. I am very thankful to each for their positive influences.

Some of my instructors in the Philippines taught methods that display the Southeast Asian roots in silat. Many techniques of Antonio "Tatang" Ilustrisimo and grandmaster Roberto Labaniego have the lines and flavor derived from silat lineage. My sincere gratitude goes to them, as well.

I again thank tuhon Dan Inosanto for hosting so many different silat instructors at the Inosanto Academy of Martial Arts and for facilitating my training with Herman and Paul.

Finally, I am indebted to my linguistic adviser Yuri Amadin (Yurimag.com) for his help with much of the terminology used in this endeavor. And many thanks to the suppliers who contributed equipment to the photo shoot: Macho.com for helmets, Revgear.com for focus mitts and gloves, and Karambit.com for karambits.

Dan Inosanto

Herman Suwanda

Paul de Thouars

Special thanks to my wonderful, very accomplished and highly skilled students (from left to right, Israel Cruz, Scott Ishihara and Jarlo Ilano) who assisted me with the photos and videos.

INTRODUCTION

PENCAK VERSUS SILAT

Our understanding of principles greatly affects our effectiveness in life and in the fighting arts. From my perspective, the biggest error in the *silat* community is that many don't fully understand the difference between the two words *pencak* and silat. We need to fully understand this difference and how it impacts our training if we want to be truly functional-silat fighters.

The word pencak indicates the performance-art side of the coin. This artistic expression includes various types of dances and single or multiple-person forms. It is an integral part of Southeast Asian martial training, but the emphasis is on being aesthetically pleasing.

Silat is the fight. A fight is when your partner or opponent is actively fighting back against you. Silat takes place during sparring practice, fighting competition or actual combat. It is the application of the art against someone who is resisting your every move.

Long ago, actual fighting practice was almost always taught at the same time as or even before the dance portion. Knowing how to fight made the dance more meaningful. But over time, the demonstration side took precedence, often at the expense of sparring. While pencak is great for developing strength, agility, flexibility, coordination, relaxation and grace, it is no substitute for silat practice if you are preparing for combat. This is one of the main points that I want to emphasize in this book. If you want to be able to actually use your silat, you need to go beyond just practicing the pencak. You need to work with a partner who is not cooperating with you.

The big misunderstanding occurs because many (not all) silat practitioners think that training their entries, strikes and takedowns on a cooperative partner is the silat portion of the art. But that is not correct. If you go through fast, ferocious routines and your partner is cooperating with you, then you are practicing highly energetic pencak. Silat means to fight, and there is no fight unless your partner is resisting you.

Here's a motto that I devised years ago that is apropos: "If you want to learn how to fight, you must practice fighting against someone who is fighting back." That is what the silat portion of the training covers. Going through techniques on a cooperative partner is simply another form of dance, regardless of how viciously you apply your techniques. That is not to say that pencak practice is useless. Indeed, it is very valuable for ingraining proper form, attitude and technique while working on physical and mental qualities essential to fighting. But some fighting attributes are only gained through sparring. Reading a crafty opponent's intentions, proper timing and developing the determination to overcome obstacles are only learned in the crucible of combat. Training against a resisting partner during your silat practice is crucial to fighting success, and the pencak portion reinforces this practice.

Please remember that sparring shouldn't be an all-out affair. In Thai boxing, which is a derivative of silat, fighters spar at about 60 percent intensity most of the time. They do many rounds of light sparring and go all-out on the Thai pads and during their matches. Sparring hard is dangerous, and it does not pay to go into a fight injured. Do your sparring, but do it safely, at moderate intensity and under the supervision of a qualified instructor. This is what most silat practitioners did for many millennia. The resistance can be minimal, but it forces you to spontaneously find solutions to problems, and that is what being functional in fighting and life is all about.

The pencak portion is very important for ingraining moves, working on physical attributes and enhancing your health. The *kembangan* (flower dance), for example, is enjoyable, and the dance keeps the body and mind supple and healthy. For longevity and vitality, the dances are extremely practical. Practicing *jurus* (one-person forms) helps ingrain fighting motions as you practice your lever positions and footwork patterns. If you are a pencak silat practitioner who also wants to keep the practical fighting portion of the art alive, please grasp and pass on this vitally important concept: *Only when your partner is truly resisting your techniques are you engaging in silat.*

The flower dance — this is an example of the pencak portion of the art.

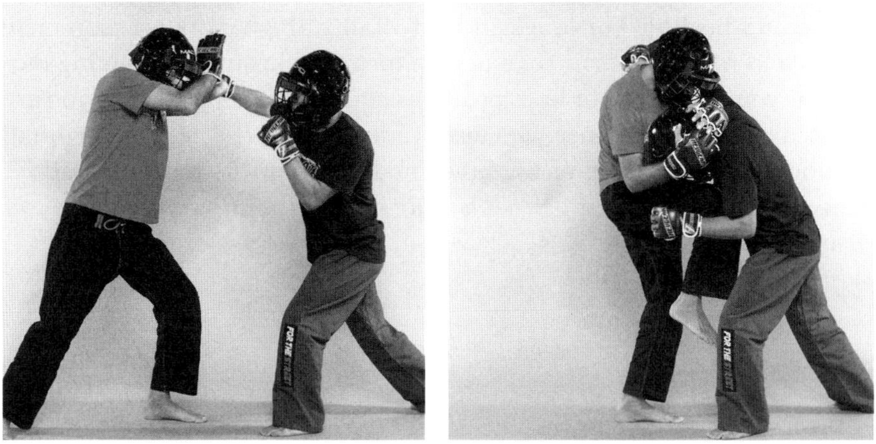

Sparring sequence against a partner who is fighting back — this is the silat portion of the art.

SILAT IN THE MMA ERA

After diligently training in silat, I found that it worked very well for me. As one of the original Dog Brothers (I earned the moniker Lucky Dog), I often used silat during all-out, minimal-protection stick fights. Although our style of stick fighting was deemed "too extreme" by original Ultimate Fighting Championship promoter Art Davie, I was able to regularly apply foot sweeps, my go-to move the *tarik kepala* (head tilt) takedown, along with other techniques. In fact, tarik kepala worked so well in these all-out affairs that after some time, a couple of my fellow Dog Brothers took me aside and asked me to stop using it because they were afraid someone was going to get hurt.

I also used silat in stick-fighting tournaments, in a challenge stick match in the Philippines and in two empty-hand challenge matches. When people questioned the effectiveness of silat, some teachers pointed to my fighting success as proof that the approach really worked. Then came MMA.

It was still called no-holds barred in the mid-1990s when I started training and sparring with some of the first high-level NHB fighters, particularly with the Inoue brothers, Egan and Enson. I was in for a shock. I couldn't get my silat to work against athletes with a strong grappling background. Sure, I wasn't kicking them in the groin or gouging their eyes, but we must acknowledge that our blows aren't always going to land or have a significant effect. I just couldn't break the posture enough to get to a good sweep or takedown. This was frustrating because I knew silat worked. I had used it against fully resisting opponents many times. But this was a different world. The grapplers' base was just too stable, and I couldn't do the head tilt because their necks were too strong and set. To make it worse, I found that my stance was vulnerable to wrestling takedowns.

After more than a year of trying and failing, I decided to put silat aside. It was a sad and difficult decision. I enjoyed a fine reputation as a silat fighter in addition to receiving accolades in *jeet kune do* and *kali.* But for me, the truth always comes first. My main purpose was (and is) to be the most effective fighter I could be and then pass my understanding of functional-skill development on to my students. Silat wasn't working well, so I had to move on.

I put most of my energy into mixed martial arts and Brazilian *jiu-jitsu* while still doing functional kali, JKD and *muay Thai.* The No. 1 lesson I learned from working with various MMA champions is that the training method really is most important for functional-skill development. You must train against a resisting opponent or you will never be able to apply your technique against a real aggressor. That's when I coined that phrase, "If you want to learn how to fight, you must practice fighting against someone who is fighting back!" Technique is very important, but being able to apply your technique, even if you have only mastered a few, is paramount. As one of my BJJ instructors John Machado says, "No sparring, no miracles!"

Over the next decade, I eventually earned my black belt in BJJ and became a top-level MMA and grappling coach, leading fighters at the UFC and elite grappling events. But something was still missing. After immersing myself for more than a decade in the sport, I came up for a breath and realized that I had been neglecting street-specific tactics. MMA definitely worked, and a good MMA fighter would almost always prevail in a one-on-one street fight. But we all know that there are no rules on the street. Because street self-defense effectiveness was my primary aim, I put the groin strikes, throat grabs and simulated eye attacks back into sparring. We did it safely, but we trained these tactics with resistance. And guess what? Things changed again.

You train to create habits. If you don't train to defend against foul tactics, they are going to get through your sport defense if the adversary is also skilled at real fighting. Some sport advocates say they would just make a mental adjustment if fighting in the street, but what would cue your sport-trained subconscious that you were in a street fight? A swift kick to the groin or a thumb in the eye. Some will say, and I agree, that those shots won't stop them. But an armbar won't stop you in a life-and-death fight, either, so why practice defending against that? If you want to train for self-defense, train with the rules of the street: no rules.

Something else happened as I opened myself back up to techniques not usually practiced in the sport. I was sparring with longtime training partner David Giomi in Hawaii. We were in the clinch, I made a move, he countered, and then I countered back and flowed into a silat technique. Hmm. A few days later, we were sparring in the clinch again, David made a good countermove to my arm-drag attempt and I caught him in a cross-arm-lock trap/throw. An hour before that, I would have said that the cross-arm lock is great for movies but basically impossible to use against someone who is fighting back. But it worked against a very skillful fighter. I got it again later and subsequently against many of my students during vigorous sparring sessions. What had happened?

First, I realized that most silat techniques work in the clinch. Typically, the silat fighter makes a strong entry with a strike to stun the opponent, then moves directly to a takedown. But what if the strike doesn't have an effect? You are going to be in the clinch and have to go back to striking. But he is going to be hitting, too. I found that if you are skilled in the clinch, which comes from lots of clinch sparring in which strikes are included, you can nullify the opponent's strikes and then look for favorable striking or positioning to set up a hard throw, including those found in silat. Being proficient in the clinch is vital against an MMA-trained fighter.

How about off-balancing those big wrestlers in the clinch? The street tactics solved that problem. If I am proficient in the clinch, I can maneuver myself into position to grab an opponent's throat and lift him onto his toes. That makes him easy to maneuver into a throw. Slap the opponent's groin, even when he is wearing protection, and he will usually bend over. These tactics put your partner in a vulnerable position, opening him up to numerous techniques. Because throat grabs and groin slaps can be done safely in sparring, you can get that all-important fighting experience against someone who is actually fighting back.

So becoming skillful in MMA opened the door to me reintroducing and applying silat techniques by using setups that are outside the rules of the sport. That eventually led to the Silat for the Street program.

Sadly, this kind of resistance training is not the norm anymore in most silat approaches. It not only keeps the students and instructors from becoming highly functional, but pencak-only training also leads many far down the path of fantastical hypothesis.

Currently, when most people train in silat techniques, the feeder throws a punch and then stands like a statue while the other practitioner goes through a long series of strikes, breaks, throws and ground finishes. Let me remind you that *anything* can work on someone who is standing still for you. Adding to the problem, the feeder is often so incredibly compliant that he will literally fall for anything. I've seen silat instructors make the feeder collapse like a house of cards in a stout wind by poking him in the back of the knee. That may work if you have a knife in your hand, but it isn't going to get you any results when just using your finger.

Some have claimed that silat has always been a dead art and that I just took the principle of resistance training from JKD or MMA and applied it to silat. But who first brought home to me the importance of working with an uncooperative partner? It was *pak* Herman Suwanda in the mid-1980s. We were practicing a defense for a two-handed choke from the front. He demonstrated on me. I grasped his throat with both hands, and then he took his fingers, stuck them into the base of my trachea and pressed down hard. I released my grip immediately. While I was practicing this over and over with my partner, Herman came to me and said, "Do it to me." He put his hands around my neck, and I pressed my fingers into his trachea. He let go and said, "Good, one more time." He again grabbed me by the neck. Just as I started to reach for his trachea, he squeezed and started shaking me all over the place. I was so busy trying to get my bearings and catch my balance that I couldn't even think about doing the counter. After a few long seconds, he stopped and gave me that big Herman smile. "Different, isn't it?" he asked.

If you want to be able to apply your silat in a real situation, then you must regularly train against a partner who is providing authentic resistance. With safe sparring, you can learn how to flow and apply the amazing art of silat against someone who is fighting back.

CHAPTER ONE

FUNCTIONAL-SILAT PRINCIPLES

There are hundreds of principles in *silat,* but we only have room in this book for a few. Here are some of the most important principles for functional fighting.

BE HONEST

If you aren't honest with yourself, you will never admit your faults, which means you will never have cause to improve them. Teachers who are not honest with students will allow them to think that they are better than they are, which can be dangerous in a real situation. Honest training in which partners counter each other's moves results in honest assessment and improvement.

ASSUME ALL ATTACKERS ARE ARMED

In silat, you should assume that every fight is a knife fight — the attacker is hiding a blade or is going to draw a weapon during the encounter. This influences the urgency of your defense so you finish the fight as quickly as possible. You also must ensure that the aggressor's arms are always accounted for so you can recognize the draw and deal with the weaponry threat early. If you can't see or feel the combatant's arms, you can't detect a weapon being drawn.

USE FORWARD PRESSURE

This means you take the fight to the attacker both physically and mentally. You drive forward using your leverage while striking and overwhelming the attacker with your physical technique. You do your best to constantly move forward with maximum pressure in order to keep the aggressor off-balance and looking for a way out.

You also keep pressuring with your relentless fighting spirit. Your determination is palpable, which can diminish the will of the attacker.

USE LEVERAGE AND LEVER POSITIONS

Leverage is aligning your skeletal structure in a way to maximize your body's strength. This is not about muscle power, although it does help. Your posture should be in the strongest possible position to apply that force against the weakest structure of the attacker. Maximize your leverage while minimizing that of the aggressor.

The farther a weight is from the fulcrum, the more leverage you must generate to lift that weight. Use leverage to optimize your technique, especially against a larger foe. The farther you put your weight from the attacker's core, the weaker he or she is. When grabbing to set up strikes or takedowns, grasp limbs in areas that compromise the opponent's leverage. Push higher on an attacker's forehead to lessen the person's leverage to fight the move.

There are two basic, but valuable, lever positions from which you can maximize your skeletal structure to exert maximum force.

The forward-lever position is the "pushing the car" posture in which your feet are nearly in a straight line and you bend at the waist to get your nose approximately over your lead foot. Maintain good posture in your lower back. If you have to push a car, you will naturally get into the forward lever because it is the strongest position you can assume while moving forward.

The side-lever position is the "breaking down the door" posture in which you lean to the side, leading with your shoulder. The idea here is to ram the attacker with your shoulder, usually after stepping inside the attack. You also can use a side lever in a twist stance.

Forward-lever position

Side-lever position

BE AN ANCHOR

An attacker's common counter to a sweep is simply to lift the leg being swept and step out. But the attacker can't step out if you anchor him by using your weight to hang on his arm, neck or body to tilt him and keep the weight on the leg you want to sweep. Unable to stay balanced and step away, the attacker will go down when you sweep the leg.

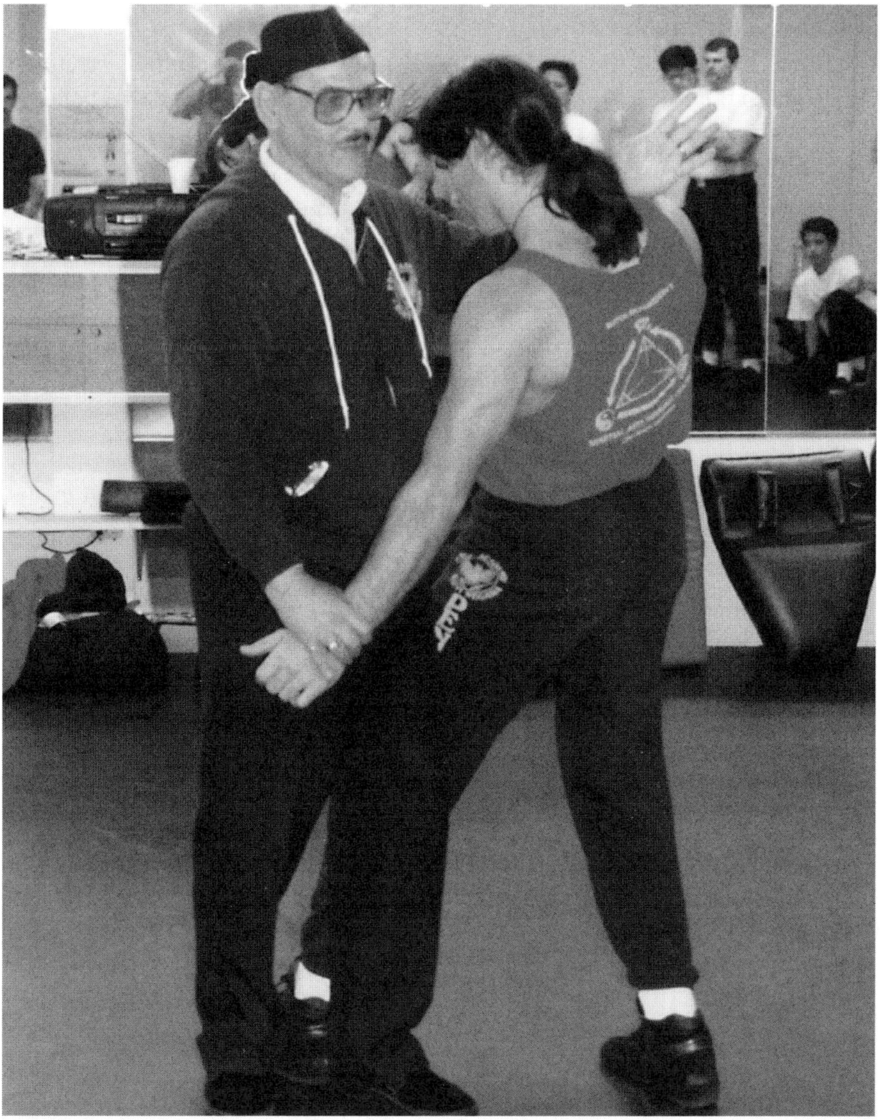

Paul de Thouars and Burton Richardson demonstrate the anchor position.

OBSERVE TRIANGLE BASELINE THEORY

Draw a line between your partner's feet. Use that as a baseline to make two equilateral triangles, one with the point in front of the opponent and the other with the point behind the opponent. These are the partner's two weakest points for off-balancing. Pushing along the baseline allows the opponent to easily resist. However, making the opponent move toward the point of either triangle requires the opponent to take a step to maintain balance. Off-balancing toward the rear triangle is preferable because the opponent has little upper-body flexibility in that direction. When you move him toward the front triangle, he may bend at the waist to catch his balance.

OFF-BALANCE THE OPPONENT

Menggoyah means to disrupt or off-balance an opponent. In the process, you also must maintain your balance. This can be physical and/or mental. A solid, rooted aggressor — especially one trained in MMA or grappling — is difficult to take down. A heavy attacker naturally has a strong base. Menggoyah is the art of either shifting the attacker to one foot or up on his toes. Even a heavy attacker on tiptoes or balanced on one foot will move easily, facilitating takedowns.

Like the grappling sports, silat does use pushing and pulling to manipulate the assailant's balance. But silat relies more heavily on throat grabs, eye gouges and groin attacks to off-balance a bigger, stronger aggressor. This is extremely important to functional silat, especially when defending against a trained fighter.

If you want to be a formidable fighter, your mental base must be extremely stable so that you can withstand any and all setbacks. You must develop your fighting spirit so it is very difficult for someone to shake those important mental attributes of courage, determination, confidence and persistence. In a fight, you want to disrupt the aggressor's mental base as well as the physical. Yelling, displaying a confident attitude, overwhelming with forward pressure and strikes, employing a hard takedown or even breaking a limb can cause an assailant to lose the will to fight. Once the attacker's spirit is broken, victory is yours.

"MAKE A WAY"

When moving into position to take down an attacker, you must maintain your own strong leverage position while diminishing the adversary's. The problem is that the aggressor is in your way. It is natural to move your body offline to get around the attacker, but this gives away your leverage advantage. Instead, you must, as *pendekar* Paul de Thouars would say, "Make a way." This means that you move the attacker's body out of position while moving in with a strong lever position. Silat fighters must be disciplined to maintain their own leverage when entering. If you can't make a way, change tactics and go for another position that you can use without compromising your structure.

Burton Richardson has proper grips and needs to "make a way" in order to step behind Scott Ishihara's leg (1). Richardson keeps pressure on the throat and anchors the arm to push Ishihara's upper body back to make space to step through (2). Richardson uses pressure on the throat to turn and throw Ishihara to the ground (3-5).

USE PRECISE ANGLES

You can sweep an attacker using power, but you always want to maximize your efficiency so that the techniques work against larger people. Using precise angles on sweeps and throws is what gives silat much of its seemingly magic qualities. When you hit the move just right, the techniques feel effortless.

RECOGNIZE THE ATTACKER'S BASIC BODY POSTURES

A standing attacker is going to be in one of three basic postures: very upright, slightly bent forward with bent knees in an athletic position or bent over at the waist. Recognizing these postures is important because each one is vulnerable to specific attacks and takedowns. If your favorite takedown is the head tilt, then you are going to need to get the attacker upright in order to apply it. These postures will be referenced and further explained throughout the book.

Thoughts on Exotic Postures

During kickboxing sparring rounds at *tuhon* Dan Inosanto's class one evening in the late 1980s, I was paired with a *jeet kune do* man from the early days. This was his first group class in several years, so he had no knowledge of *silat.* After we began, Inosanto shouted out to me, "Burt, sit down!" I understood what he wanted, as I had been experimenting for months employing silat postures during sparring. I waved my hands in the air and moved back into the *sempok* sitting position. The JKD man dropped his hands, gave me a look of utter disgust, then stepped forward to kick me in the head — exactly what I wanted. As the kick came in, I leaned forward to choke the power while catching the leg and standing up. I took a step forward, and he went crashing to the ground. Inosanto was pleased. It was a good lesson for both me and for my very accomplished partner. Exotic postures can actually be dangerous if you don't understand what they are for.

USE EXOTIC POSTURES

Silat is known for its exotic postures, but these are not just for show. You can use these stances to intimidate, draw an attack or to hide your attacking intentions.

Defending yourself is infinitely easier if you know what the attacker is going to throw at you. These postures may look very strange to an MMA fighter, but they can lure an unwitting assailant into a trap.

1

2

3

4

Burton Richardson sits in sempok to invite the head kick (1). Jarlo Ilano takes the bait. Richardson moves forward while checking the kick before it picks up too much steam (2), stands while catching the kick (3) and lifts Ilano's leg high for a heavy throw (4).

DEVELOP FLOW

You cannot assume that your first attempt at disabling an attacker is going to work. This is why you need to develop flow. A real attacker will be moving and resisting, so you need to be able to flow around the obstacles he imposes to achieve your goal. This is why silat is often practiced in combinations rather than as one move followed by resetting. You need to be able to put the attacker on the defense and flow from move to move until you achieve the position to finish the fight. Flow allows you to spontaneously overcome obstacles and find solutions. Apply this principle in your everyday life, as well.

EMPHASIZE PUKULAN PENCAK SILAT

Pukulan means striking with a fist. Pukulan is often added before *pencak silat* in order to highlight the emphasis on striking. The pukulan arts are not just about moving in and then throwing and controlling the adversary on the ground. Striking is essential during the entry, is used to set up the takedown and is the primary form of neutralizing a downed attacker. For functional self-defense, strikes must be integrated into all phases of the silat continuum.

HAVE THREE SHARP KNIVES

There is a saying among Southeast Asian fighters that you should always have three knives with you for self-defense: one to use, one to throw and one to give to a friend. And they must all be very sharp! This saying is also used to describe the concept of having three primary moves that are your go-to techniques. It's fine to know a lot of entries and takedowns, but you should have a few so thoroughly practiced that you can apply them on almost anyone without thought. And where do you find out which moves work best for you? Through sparring. If you spar enough, you will discover your own proclivities.

Find your top three moves and hone them until they are extremely sharp. You should still take time to practice the other moves in case the opportunity to apply them arises, but be sure to have your favorite "blades" honed to a razor's edge.

ATTACK THE MOST VULNERABLE TARGETS

It is easy in this world of combat sports to forget that, as painful as they are, Thai kicks to the thigh and punches to the head often take time to produce an effect. A groin kick usually works right away. Fingers in the eyes, kicking the side of the knee and striking the throat are illegal in combat sports because they injure the combatant and the fight ends too quickly. But that is exactly what you want in self-defense. Keep in mind that you should always be looking to use the moves that most efficiently inflict the greatest damage on a larger, stronger, determined attacker who means to do bodily harm.

1

2

3

Burton Richardson parries Israel Cruz's jab (1) and throws a devastating cross-stomp kick (2), which goes to the very vulnerable side of the knee (3), a move that is illegal in combat sports.

CHAPTER TWO

SILAT WEAPONRY AND EMPTY-HAND TECHNIQUES

Silat is a blade art that also has empty-hand fighting methods. This book focuses on the empty-handed approach, but some of silat's often-misconstrued concepts should also be discussed.

Although it is true that many empty-hand moves are derived from weaponry techniques, it should be clear that just because a tactic works with a weapon does not mean that it is functional with empty hands. Teachers sometimes proclaim that any move you can do with a weapon can be applied equally as well without a weapon, but that is not accurate. Slashing downward at the attacker's hand with a sword has a very different effect than doing the same move with an open hand. Some functional-knife movements, such as rapid combinations of slashing and thrusting, are actually dangerous when applied empty-handed. The slashes with the knife may effectively disable the incoming knife arm, but attacking in the same way empty-handed leaves you open to being clocked by the aggressor's other hand.

While the weaponry movements are important, you must realize that some don't translate to empty hands as well as others. There are many instances in which weapon-based motions can be translated to efficient empty-handed techniques. You should thoroughly understand which are functional and which can put you in danger. Here are a few examples of movements that work with a blade but can be problematic without one.

KARAMBIT VS. EMPTY-HAND TECHNIQUES

Example A

Armed

The karambit is a Southeast Asian knife used for extreme self-defense. Here is an example of an upward motion with the karambit attacking the biceps (1), followed by a horizontal backhand slash to the throat (2).

1

2

3

Empty-Handed

Doing the same motions empty-handed, substituting the elbow for the knife, is possible but nowhere near as effective and presents dangers. An upward strike with the elbow to the biceps may hurt but will rarely disable an aggressive attacker (1). The horizontal back elbow leaves an opening for Scott Ishihara to move to Burton Richardson's back (2-3).

Example B

Armed

As Scott Ishihara steps in, Burton Richardson pulls out a karambit (1). Richardson traps Ishihara's right foot with his left while leaning to the side and hooking the blade inside Ishihara's knee, where the ligaments are located (2). Richardson continues falling to the side, pulling Ishihara to the ground while potentially inflicting tremendous damage (3). This karambit move is frighteningly effective.

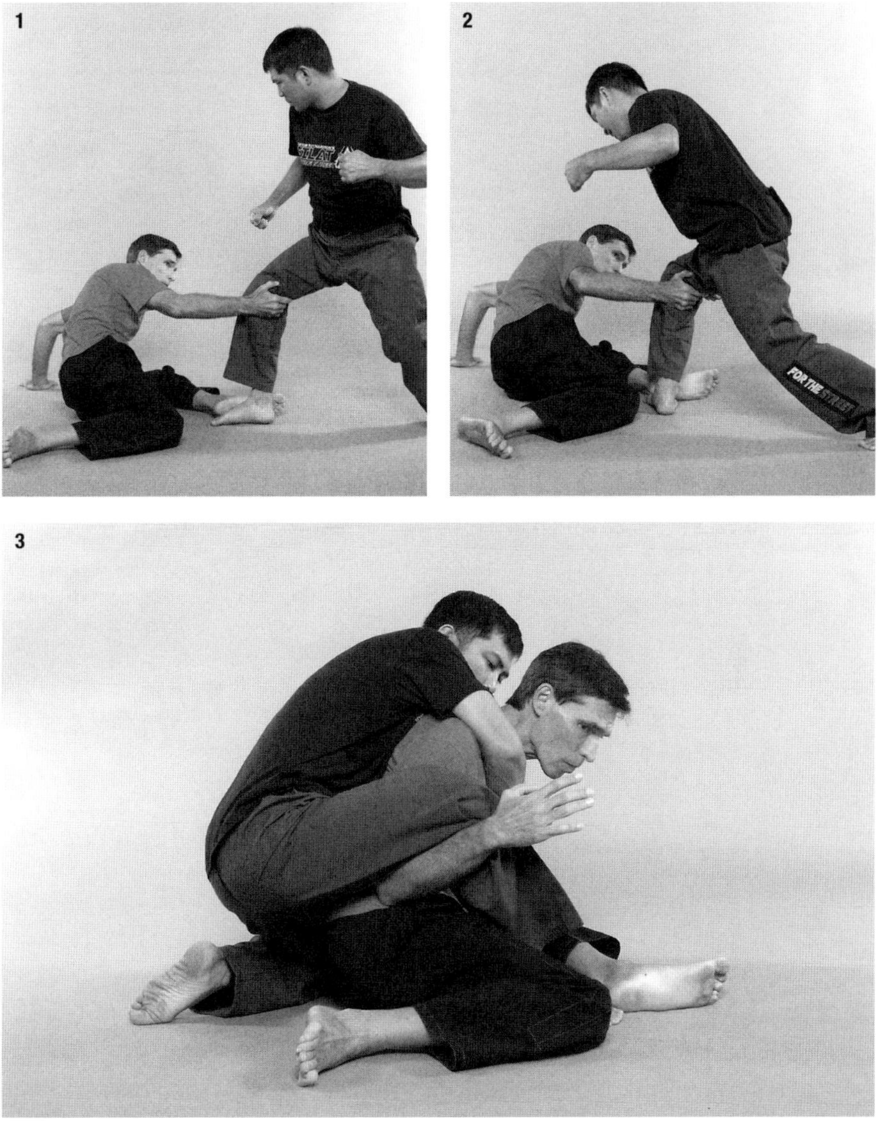

Empty-Handed

Doing the knee pull empty-handed is a different story. Burton Richardson traps Scott Ishihara's foot, grips the ligaments with his fingers and starts to pull (1). But if Ishihara is able to rotate his foot toward the pull, he counters the takedown (2) and has the opportunity to jump to Richardson's back while trapping an arm (3). Although the knee pull can work, it does pose dangers: Besides being on the ground against a standing, striking attacker, you also can end up in a compromised grappling position.

CHAPTER THREE

MULTIPLE ATTACKERS

Fighting one-on-one is tough enough, but having multiple attackers is extremely difficult for anyone. It isn't like the movies in which the bad guys are professional stuntmen who are paid to make the star look good. It is a nightmare situation to have to face a ruthless, vicious, real-world mob mentality.

Your best tactic is to find or create an escape route and use it. Use your training to maneuver yourself into a position in which you can do your best impression of an Olympic sprinter! If you can't escape or if you're with someone you need to protect, you must be more aggressive, more skillful and smarter than the attackers.

Here are a couple of the best silat answers for a multiple-opponent situation.

PULL AN EQUALIZER

A mob attack leaves you at such a disadvantage that pulling out an equalizer is usually legally justified. Before ever having to face such a situation, though, be sure to consult with your local law officials to be certain that whatever you are carrying and how you are carrying it is legal. You also should know where self-defense crosses over the line to criminal assault. This is especially true when using weapons against unarmed assailants.

In silat culture, producing a knife is not just fair but highly encouraged. You can use it to threaten and intimidate the crowd or, if necessary, go on the attack to make them stop. You must read the situation and determine what actions are necessary to protect yourself and your loved ones.

If you are forced to engage, keep moving and be extremely aggressive. Be ferocious. Don't let anyone get behind you, and protect your knife arm from being grabbed. Throw out a volley of strong, fast combinations to keep the attackers at bay. Most bullies are cowards and don't want to deal with any resistance, especially in the form of a blade. Knowing how to brandish the knife may be enough to dissuade the attackers. If not, make your attacks precise, properly targeted and deceptive. Get in, get the job done and get out. Escape as soon as you can.

Knowing how to wield a knife can intimidate and dissuade a group of empty-handed attackers.

ATTACK THE FARTHEST AGGRESSOR AND GET OUTSIDE THE CIRCLE

When being threatened by several aggressors, one of them usually will be the leader, the head bully. He is the one who is doing the talking, being the tough guy. Often, some of the others aren't totally on board with the bullying but are too weak to say anything, so they lag behind in the back.

One common approach in this situation is to "take out the mouth," meaning you attack the leader, hoping that by hurting that attacker, the others will run away. One drawback to that method is that if it doesn't go as planned, the others will collapse inward and mob you. In the silat approach, you go after the aggressor who is the farthest away from you.

Instead of attacking the main aggressor, make a sudden burst toward the farthest bully and crack him while you run past him. By suddenly going after the person who least expects to be attacked, you enjoy the element of surprise. You go after an easy, unprotected target and get yourself outside the circle so the others can't converge on you. This gives you a big head start, and hopefully you can outrun the rest of the assailants.

In this scenario, there is one main aggressor and two friends backing him up. When Burton Richardson believes that an attack is imminent (1), he suddenly bursts toward the farthest, least-prepared fighter, hitting him as he runs (2). This counterattack puts Richardson outside the circle and gives him an escape route with a head start.

As with all other aspects of silat training, it is imperative that you practice multiple-opponent scenarios with resisting opponents. Use progressive resistance and good safety equipment, making sure that nobody gets wild. As you drill, do your best to keep from being surrounded and keep circling to try to get the attackers in a line so you only deal with one at a time. If they surround you, use the ram's horn defense and run through the middle like a football fullback crashing through the line. Hit and move, hit and move, until you can escape.

With trustworthy partners, you can take the intensity up quite a bit without undue risk of injury. Be sure to have an experienced instructor there to regulate the intensity of the rounds. Playing the various performance games with multiple opponents will surely open your eyes to the reality of the situation, as it is never easy.

Progressive Resistance and Variable Intensity

People often get squeamish at the thought of training with resistance, as they envision a hulking opponent smashing them repeatedly in the face — not a pretty picture. In fact, it is one I have been on the receiving end of. I had been boxing for about a year when my coach set up a sparring session with Randall "Tex" Cobb's bodyguard at the old Main Street Gym in downtown Los Angeles. This guy was huge and weighed in at nearly 300 pounds. My coach told him to take it easy because he had boxed professionally. Unfortunately, some people have a hard time turning the intensity down. (This is why we make sure that our students are paired up with others who want to train at the same level of intensity. We also use helmets.)

I moved around with him, and he unleashed a jab that I distinctly remember to this day. Let's just say that I learned the difference between having my hands up under my chin and really having my hands up in front of my face. That thunderous jab drove me back into the ropes, almost off my feet. Up went my hands, and boy did my head start moving. So did my feet. I was all over that ring. Luckily, I was in better shape and he tired out with about 30 seconds left in the round.

Most people will never go back to training after getting a headache like that. My coach was so encouraging that I didn't give up. But that is the normal method in boxing gyms. Many professional coaches first want to see whether prospective fighters have heart, so they toss them in the ring with a pro to see how they handle the beating. If they have heart, they will train them so they can try to make a living off them.

I want to give the realistic training to everyone, so I employ the concept of "progressive resistance." I got this term from bodybuilding, and I like to use a weightlifting analogy to explain this principle. Imagine that you decide to sign up at a gym. (Martial arts sounded too dangerous!) You have a personal trainer teach you how to lift correctly and get you going in the right direction. You tell the trainer that you want to work on your leg strength. She says OK and teaches you how to do a squat. She puts a broomstick across your shoulders, feet shoulder-width apart, and your back kept straight while you bend at the knees. She points out that you should sit back, almost like sitting in a chair, to avoid having your knees move out in front of your toes — better for your knees and better for balance. After a few minutes, you can duplicate the squat correctly. Now, what did you actually just learn? You learned a technique. That would be like going to our JKD Unlimited/MMA for the Street class and learning how to throw a solid punch. It has taken you about three minutes to learn the proper form for the technique called the squat.

Now what happens? Do you just practice that technique with the broomstick for the next three years? No. Your trainer takes you to the squat rack. Why? Because you need to add resistance if you want to get stronger. Doing the technique with resistance is going to trigger the "adaptive response." If you don't add resistance, you are not going to get stronger. If you don't add resistance in your fight training, you won't develop fighting skill. Let's now say that your wonderful trainer takes you to the squat rack and proceeds to load the bar with 300 pounds. What is going to happen if you try to squat that much your first day? You are going to break something. Why? Too much resistance! You have to start with just enough resistance to make the effort slightly difficult. This causes your body to adapt. You go in the following week and you can add a little more resistance. Over time, depending on your goals, you may be able to squat with 300 pounds.

The same theory of progressive resistance holds true for our fight training. Too much resistance is counterproductive. You will actually be worse off by adding too much resistance than not training at all. Instead, the trick is to add enough resistance so that it is slightly difficult to apply your technique. As you improve, you add more resistance.

The amount you end up training with depends on your goals. I call this "variable intensity training" because each person in class trains at his or her own level. Our rule is that when two people play together, the intensity is adjusted for whoever wants to go lighter. Some people lift weights to tone up, while others train to be bodybuilders. Some people want to train martial arts for health and self-defense, while others want to become cage-fighting champions. The amount of resistance and the level of intensity will differ depending on your goals. You may end up doing two sets of squats with 135 pounds. You stop when you start to feel the burn. A professional may build up to 400 pounds over six sets, taking many of the sets to the point at which they cannot possibly do another rep. (Those are the guys screaming in the corner of the gym.) They add more resistance at a greater level of intensity.

In our training, I can spar at full resistance, doing my best to defend each offensive attempt from my opponent without using full intensity. I can strike quickly without full power so that my partner is not overwhelmed. That way we all improve and have fun doing it.

There is one more very important aspect of this weightlifting analogy. Whether you are in the gym to tone or to become a competitive bodybuilder, the basic techniques you perform are the same. You do squats, bench presses, curls, lat pulls, etc. The professional adds greater intensity and uses more variations of each technique, but the basics are the same. This holds true for fight training, as well. The basics will be the same whether you are a hobbyist or a professional fighter. There is no need to have one curriculum for fighters and an entirely different curriculum for people who want to learn self-defense. The professional is just more skillful in the basics and has more variations. There's nothing magic about it, just scientifically tested techniques and training methods performed using progressive resistance to build that skill.

I hope you can see why progressive resistance is an extremely important part of our training. This is what allows people of all ages, sizes and goals to train in the same general manner as a winner in the Ultimate Fighting Championship. Because the concept of progressively adding more and more resistance is not widely understood, many martial arts don't include that all-important factor that triggers the adaptive response: resistance. They instead practice forms, drills and techniques in which neither person ever actually fights back.

These drills and techniques are performed without any resistance of any kind. Bruce Lee used the term "aliveness" to talk about adding resistance. This is often misinterpreted. People will take a technique that is practiced without resistance and try to make it "alive." They do this by bouncing around like Muhammad Ali while doing the technique, still without resistance. Bouncing around does not make it alive. Resistance makes it alive. Movement is part of resistance, and it is easy to confuse the two. If your partner is trying to keep you from performing your technique, then there is resistance and you are going to improve.

Intensity is also mistaken for resistance. A person can go through a technique routine with a well-trained, compliant partner at great intensity. This is wonderful in demonstrations. One person feeds and the other person flies into a fast, intense series of blocks, eye strikes and nerve hits, followed by a takedown. Very impressive. That guy was moving with unbelievable speed, precision and power. Watch the demonstration again and take note of the feeder. What you will usually see is a person who throws a punch and then stands there while the defender goes through the routine. No resistance. There is great intensity in this type of demonstration, but without resistance, you won't be able to deal with a real attacker who will resist 100 percent.

Am I saying that it is useless to train without resistance? No. Training without resistance is important to memorize the various techniques. By memorize I mean that your body has to develop the coordination for the technique so that you have all the details in place. You also can use them for conditioning the body. Just like learning the squat, you need to learn each technique. But again, like the squat, it should only take a few minutes to learn most techniques. There are only two types of drills that martial artists do: memorization drills and resistance drills. I call resistance drills "performance games." We learn the technique and then put it right into the performance game so that you develop the skill to use the technique while under pressure.

Is an attacker in the street going to resist you? Absolutely. If you don't practice with resistance, you won't be able to handle the situation. I'm going to say it again: "If you want to learn how to fight, you must practice fighting against someone who is fighting back!"

CHAPTER FOUR

FOOTWORK

Langkah (footwork) in silat is extremely important for getting to an optimal angle against an attacker. Assuming that the assailant is bigger and stronger than you are, you don't want to go force against force. Because of this, you must use evasive footwork on the outside to avoid strong attacks or use precise footwork to enter at optimal angles.

The idea is to use footwork to get into a position in which you can maximize your force and direct it against the attacker's weakest point. (See the Triangle Baseline Theory discussion in Chapter One.)

There are many complex footwork patterns, such as the *serak* diagram shown here, but remember that they are actually combinations of the basic components. Memorizing the patterns is not enough. Training to use them against a resisting attacker is most important.

The pattern applications, especially when the patterns are put into combinations, are virtually infinite. Practice them well so that you can use the art of angulation to overcome larger, stronger attackers without thought.

FOOTWORK PATTERNS

This chapter presents some of the most useful footwork patterns from silat. There are *many* applications and variations for each footwork pattern, far too many to be covered in an entire book that only covers footwork. But these will give you a great start. In combat, given that you have practiced enough, you will spontaneously combine these patterns depending on the flow of the fight.

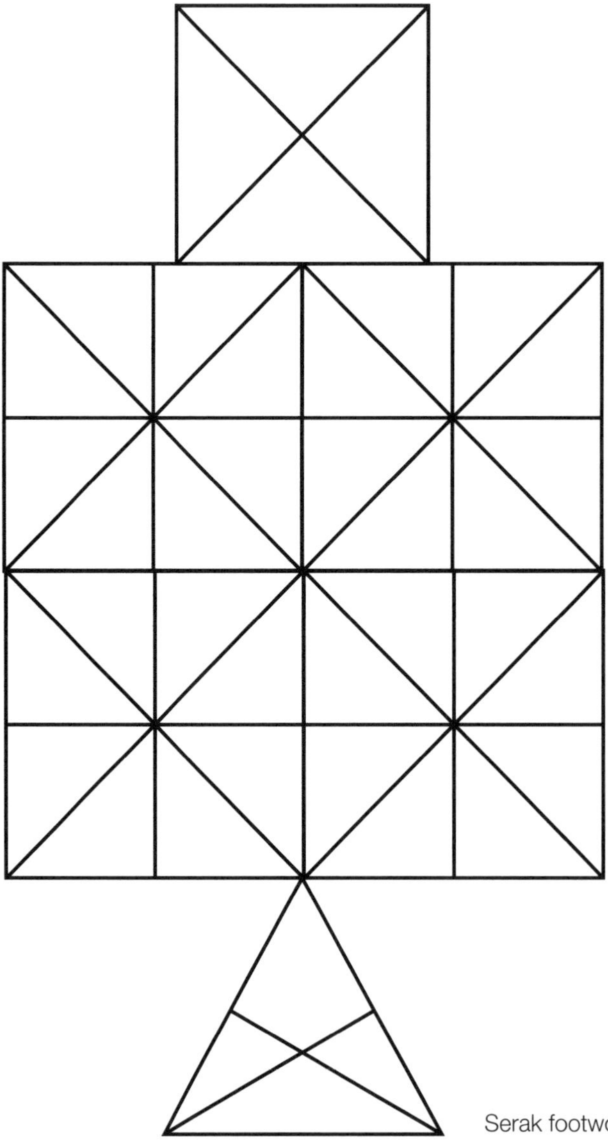

Serak footwork patterns

Dominance Through Footwork

I have a student who is a powerlifter. He is much stronger than I am and outweighs me by 70 pounds. If I go head-to-head with him, I am going to get crushed. When we spar in the clinch, my primary mission is to maneuver into a position in which I have a good angle on him. Once I achieve that angle, the size and strength disparity is eliminated and I can apply striking and other techniques with what looks like relative ease. The truth is that I am still working hard to maintain that position, but because I have the angle, I can control him and hit without being hit. Footwork is the key to getting to a dominant angle.

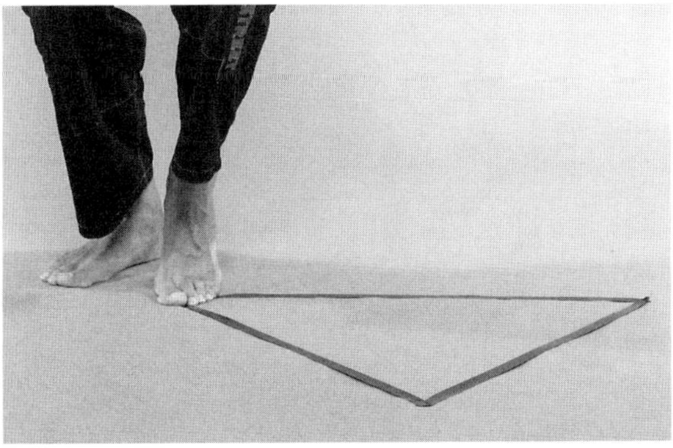

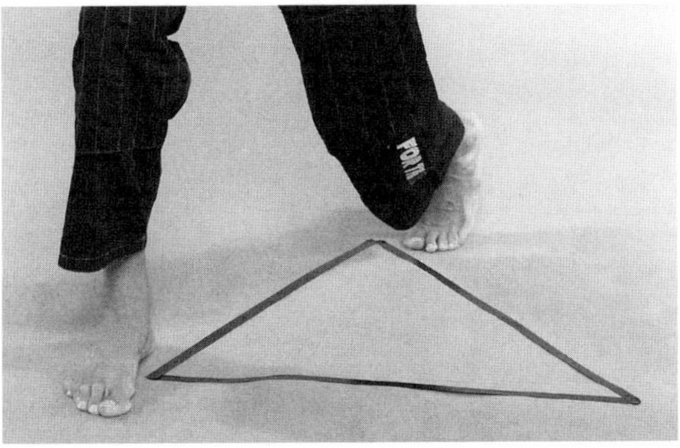

STRAIGHT LINE

This is the simplest footwork — just move straight forward. But the key is to optimize your force through using the forward-lever position. (See Lever Positions in Chapter One.) Adding the force of explosively bursting forward with the strong structure of the forward lever can overcome the force of an attacker who is more upright. This is especially useful in sudden attacks when you don't have time to use evasive movement. Straight-line footwork is usually used with the dive entry and sometimes with the flower entry (explained in Chapter Five) in order to crash in as quickly as possible.

But even when using the straight line, you don't want to go force against force like two rams butting heads. Instead, point that straight line off to the side of the attacker's centerline, usually toward his shoulder. This will give you a slight angle and allow the power of your body and legs to be directed against the outer edge of his body. You can make him turn on impact, which will off-balance him for a moment. That split second is all you need to take control of the encounter.

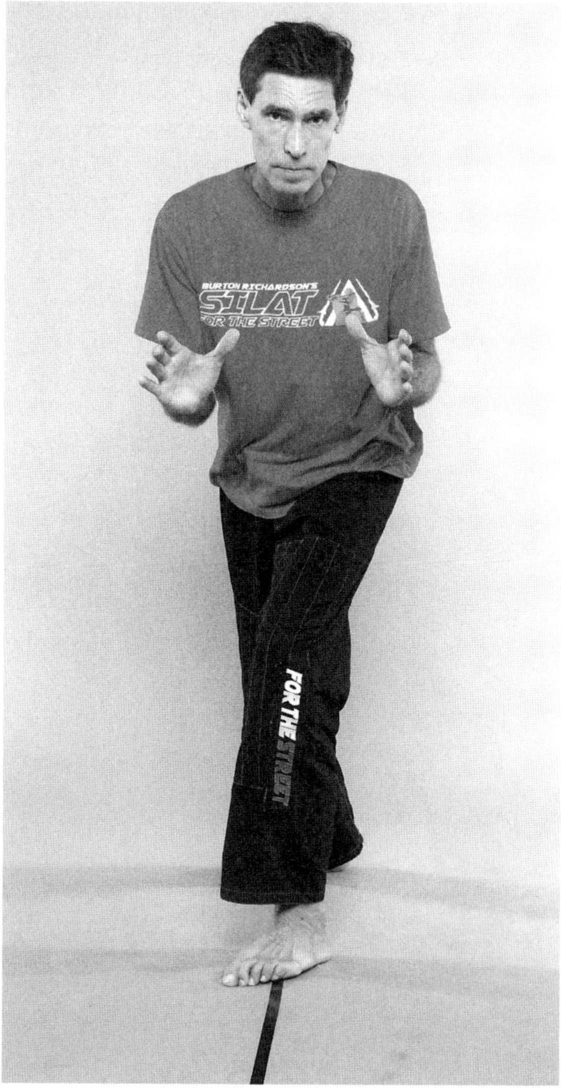

Forward-lever position on the straight line

1

2

Burton Richardson is in a ready position and Scott Ishihara loads up to fire a haymaker (1). For maximum efficiency and simplicity, Richardson steps in with the dive entry (elbow to the throat variation), using the forward lever on the straight line (2). There are myriad possible follow-ups from here.

TRIANGLE — FEMALE AND MALE

The triangle can be used outside for evasive movement, which sets up your entry at a favorable angle. There are two basic triangles: the female version, in which you are at the point of the triangle with the base in front of you, and the male version, in which you are at the base of the triangle with the point in front of you. Both are equilateral triangles, meaning the length of each side is equal and therefore each intersection angle is 60 degrees.

Because the lines are angling diagonally away from you, the female triangle lets you step to the side and forward at the same time. This means that you can evade an attack and enter simultaneously. If you step laterally to the side to evade and then try to make an entry, the aggressor may have time to fire a second blow. The female triangle allows you to enter in one beat. This is extremely efficient when entering against punches, kicks and weaponry attacks. Because the lines of the triangle point away in both directions, you can enter either inside or outside the attacker's striking arm.

The male triangle can be used to evade attacks and enter, but it is a two-step process. You step to the side and then make an angular entry. That gives an aggressive assailant two shots at you. But it is a great tactic on the outside if you want to set up an entry. The first step to the side seems like a simple flanking maneuver, but as the aggressor turns to adjust, you are already making your entry on a favorable angle. The male triangle entry is a quick, explosive movement like a juke step in football.

Forward step on the female triangle

Burton Richardson is in a neutral stance (1). Jarlo Ilano starts to swing. Richardson angles forward to the right on the female triangle to avoid the strike and get close enough to simultaneously counterstrike (2-3).

Ready to enter on the male triangle

1

2

3

Demonstrating with Israel Cruz, Burton Richardson is in a disguised ready position (1). When Cruz aggressively steps forward to shove his opponent, Richardson sidesteps to the right corner of the male triangle and drives in at an angle while slapping the aggressor's arm away and simultaneously palming his face (2-3).

SQUARE

The square is usually used for sidestepping, then moving forward or backward. If you start at the rear left corner of the square, you can sidestep to the right rear corner, then step to the forward right corner. This is very common in silat dance and in application against an aggressive attacker.

If you are at the rear left corner, you can step forward to the forward left corner with your left foot, then to the forward right corner with your right. This is used to enter and knock the attacker off-balance to the side and is essential in several takedown setups.

If you start at the forward left corner, you can step to the forward right corner with your right foot, then slide your left foot back to the rear right corner. This is used for back sweeps and for evasive movements. In *capoeira,* this footwork is called *jinga.*

Side-lever position on the square

Scott Ishihara prepares a backhand sword strike to Burton Richardson's neck (1). Richardson ducks and steps across the front line of the square (2). He then steps to the back corner of the square with his left foot (3). He leans back to evade the forehand strike (4).

LIGHTNING BOLT

The footwork you choose usually depends on the situation — how many attackers there are, where they are, what they are attacking with and where your escape route is. But to enter hard and deep against a single aggressor who is in front of you and within kickboxing range, you are usually going to use the lightning-bolt footwork. The reason is twofold; the first step has all the advantages of the female triangle. You get off the line of the incoming attack while moving closer to the aggressor. But the second step allows you to drive your shoulder, often preceded by strikes or checks, directly through the attacker toward the weakest point — the rear triangle point of the attacker's base. (See Triangle Base Theory in Chapter One.) This results in a very deep entry that drives the attacker off-balance. It also can result in a devastating takedown as your leg goes deep behind the attacker's lead leg.

The key is to twist your body slightly so that your shoulders are lined up with the second line of the lightning bolt rather than just stepping directly down the first line. That way, you use your shoulders like a battering ram with a very strong, slightly twisted side-lever position. It is a great way to enter against a skillful striker who is staying outside. Some high-level MMA fighters use this footwork. Any athlete who fights in the cage should spend a lot of time on this very valuable footwork.

Side-lever position on the lightning bolt

1

2

3

4

Burton Richardson and Jarlo Ilano square off (1). Richardson enters diagonally on the lightning bolt with a double trap (2). He transitions his right hand to Ilano's forehead while stepping deep on the lightning bolt with his right foot (3). Richardson finishes with the head tilt (4).

ASTERISK

This is a universal pattern for any motion — footwork, head movement, angles of attack for a weapon or evasive tactics. For footwork, the concept is that you are in the middle of the asterisk. From there, you can move in any direction, 360 degrees of a circle. To break it down into a more manageable pattern, eight lines are used on the asterisk so that each basic direction is covered. Once you move out along a certain line, the asterisk moves and you are once again in the center of the asterisk. You can again move in any of the eight basic directions.

This particular pattern is very important for you to learn because it also applies to your everyday life. You are always in the middle and can choose at any moment to move in any direction you like. If you have been going down a bad path, you can change right now and choose a new direction. Each direction takes you toward a particular destiny. If you are going down a path that is not best for you, change your direction and move toward a more fulfilling destination.

The asterisk can be found wherever there is movement.

TWISTING SIDE STEP

This is used to avoid a straight, committed attack — whether it's a punch, kick or sword thrust — directed toward the centerline of your body. Step to the side and rotate your body while leaning away from the incoming blow. It is a very fast movement to get off the line of the incoming assault. The twisting side step is a great tool to have in your bag in case of emergency.

1

2

3

4

5

Burton Richardson is in the ready position (1). As Jarlo Ilano begins the rear front kick, Richardson takes a step to the side with his left foot (2) and begins to twist his hips and torso while leaning away to avoid the kick. He simultaneously shelves the leg with his left arm (3). From here, Richardson can slide his right arm under the leg (4), which leads to a devastating throw (5).

Thoughts on the Twisting Side Step

I first used the twisting side step in fighting during an after-hours Dog Brothers session at the Inosanto Academy in the late 1980s. I was knife sparring with a very fast, skillful and powerful partner. We were using rattan dowels and, of course, going all-out with just head and hand protection. After going for at least 10 minutes, my back was to the heavy bags. For the first time in the round, my partner suddenly fired a vicious, rear-leg straight kick to my body as if he were trying to break me in half. It took me by surprise and I had no time to think, but my body responded. I sidestepped and twisted my body to avoid the kick while my left arm went under his calf to catch his leg. He was surprised, but not as much as I was! The spontaneous counter was because of all the years of *kali/silat* practice and having enough sparring time in that I was calm enough to allow my body to respond.

BACKWARD STEP

This is a way to quickly change direction to face a second attacker, improve your leverage for a takedown or do both at the same time. It is pretty simple — you just do an about-face and step backward. The key is to maintain a very stable position. Anytime you turn, you momentarily compromise your base, so keep your knees bent and rotate with a strong structure.

Burton Richardson is confronted by two attackers, one on each side (1). He bursts toward Scott Ishihara, going directly for the head tilt (2), while using the backward step so that he can face Israel Cruz (3). Richardson finishes the first takedown in good position to handle the next threat (4).

HARIMAU SIDE TO SIDE

This is a great way to move on the ground. The *harimau* (tiger) style is known for low postures. When the terrain is slick, it is advantageous to voluntarily start in a low position instead of slipping to the ground by accident. This footwork allows you to move while staying low and even leap at an unsuspecting attacker.

When starting from the ground first came into use, most people thought it was a strange tactic. Then the Gracies showed the world how important ground fighting is.

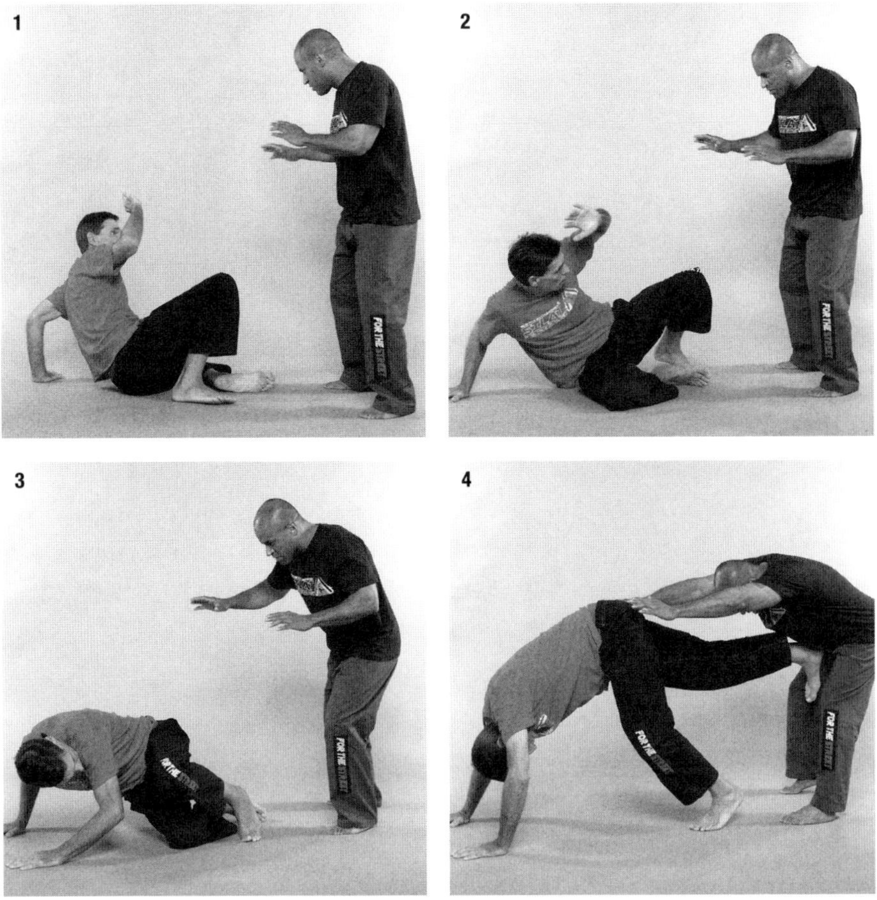

If you are already down against a standing attacker, the side-to-side movement is very useful. Burton Richardson starts leaning to the left (1). He suddenly switches to the right side, which is confusing to an attacker. Think of this like good head movement in boxing (2). The movement gives Richardson the opportunity to place his hands on the ground and throw a strong, sudden, unexpected back kick to the groin (3-4).

SEMPOK/DEPOK/SILO (TWIST STANCES)

The twist stances can be performed either standing or sitting on the ground. The twist stances are *sempok* (crossing one leg behind), *depok* (crossing one leg in front) and *silo* (just twisting into position). In Southeast Asia, people commonly sit on the ground in the sempok position, so being able to fight from there is a necessity. There are many uses for the positions, from countering back sweeps to baiting opponents to attack carelessly.

This one works well if you are late in defending the back sweep. Jarlo Ilano has gotten into good position to apply a back sweep (1-2). Because he is late, Burton Richardson's best defense is to stop Ilano's movement by controlling the head while twisting into a strong, rooted side-lever twist stance (3). Having his knee behind Ilano's leg helps Richardson finish the head-tilt takedown (4).

CHAPTER FIVE

ENTRIES

Because silat flourishes in close-quarters combat, the silat fighter needs methods to get from outside range to the inside, preferably while delivering firepower. These methods of getting to close range are "entries."

Revered Filipino martial arts grandmaster Leo Gaje once said, "The obsession of the *kali* man is how to enter." Outside, a big, aggressive, untrained attacker has a striker's chance to knock you out. Inside, it takes skill. But you need a method to go safely from outside range, through his striking power, into close range where you can use your silat. It's even better if your entry damages the attacker.

Silat entries are all about delivering firepower as you safely move to close range so you can dispatch the aggressor as quickly as possible. There are many entry methods, and their uses are situational; some work well under certain circumstances, while others work best under other conditions.

There is also overlap. There are several entries that would work against an attacker who throws a big haymaker. But remember that merely knowing the different entries does not mean that you can actually apply them under pressure. You have to drill the movements and practice against an uncooperative partner to attain the necessary timing and feel. Also, realize that even though you may know many entries, when that clenched fist is traveling violently toward your face, you only get to choose one. Have a primary response ingrained so that you can use it without thought. When things go from peaceful to violent in a split second, you will not have time to think about which method to use. Your primary response must be automatic.

Here are some of the most effective and functional entries from silat. If you want to get to close range where, as Paul de Thouars would say, "all guns can fire," then you need solid entries, preferably those that include firepower. Hone them to a fine edge so that you can dictate the range at which the fight takes place.

THE DIVE

The dive entry is a simple, universal entry. Universal means that it works against almost any type of attack: straight punches, swings, elbows, grabs and even blunt weapon attacks. The dive gets you into close quarters safely, in a hurry and with no reliance on fine-motor skills or impeccable timing.

Answering fast, powerful punches with a parry would require a lot of skill, and when an attacker suddenly pounces on you, it is very difficult to use parrying tactics. If the attack occurs at night or in low light, you may not be able to see the punches coming. The dive takes all this into account by creating a structure that protects your head as you pass through punching range into close quarters. It is so incredibly simple that its power as a self-defense tool is often overlooked.

When you feel the attacker move toward you aggressively, drop your head and extend your arms in a dive-like configuration and charge in with a forward-lever stance. The opponent's punch, elbow, bottle or rock will deflect off your arms as you slam into close range. Now you are in your territory where you can strike, clinch or go directly for a takedown.

When you dive, you will either have one arm on each side of your opponent's neck or you will have both arms on one side of his neck. This can happen by design, if you have time to think, or by chance. For example, if you favor the Thai neck clinch, you will prefer to dive with one arm on either side of the neck so that you are already set to attain the position. But in a surprise attack, you dive and flow from wherever you are.

In the dive, it is very important to keep a slight bend in your elbows so your forearms are in a diagonal line when you enter. If your forearms are horizontal, your arms may slide over the aggressor's shoulder and he can grab you in a body lock or end up at your back. Keep your elbows down so they touch the attacker's upper chest. This will surprise the attacker, stop the person's forward momentum and keep the person in front of you.

When doing the basic version, you should move into a strong forward-lever position and shock the attacker with the impact of the dive. You also can alter the structure to deliver firepower during the entry. A simple adjustment is to bend the inside arm so that you deliver a forearm or elbow strike with the dive.

You also can use the dive structure to slam your palms into the face of the aggressor, possibly driving your thumbs to the eyes, as well. It is a fast, simple, extremely damaging way to enter that doesn't take a high level of skill. But it does require lots of safe, realistic practice so you respond automatically. The dive entry should be one of your most practiced moves.

It is tempting to only practice the more complicated entries, or those that cross the line into being performance art that only works with a cooperative partner. But if you are training yourself and your students for functional self-defense, be sure to work your basics each session.

1

2

3

Burton Richardson sees that Scott Ishihara is attacking with a stick (1). Richardson confronts the attack by dropping his chin and preparing for the dive entry (2), using both palms on Ishihara's face for a jarring impact (3).

Thoughts on the Dive Entry

During a JKD Unlimited instructor test (which consists of seven rounds of sparring in all the ranges), the attacker picked up a stick and charged the instructor candidate, who spontaneously used the dive entry with the forearm smash. It is a good thing that we use extremely sturdy helmets with face cages because the forearm blow made a tremendous impact, turning the attacker's head and rattling him.

I also want to mention that my friend, practical self-defense expert Tony Blauer, developed tactics he calls the SPEAR System that are very similar in structure to the dive entry. Blauer's work demonstrating how the SPEAR System can be used in conjunction with the flinch response during surprise attacks really helped me appreciate the value of the dive entry. Blauer has refined the SPEAR System, and I highly suggest that students study his work. His psychological and physical understanding of true surprise combat is invaluable. I thank him for his contribution.

RAM'S HORN

This is similar in function to the dive entry but has a different structure. Instead of extending your arms, you cover both sides of your head as you make your entry. This instinctive move keeps you more covered than the dive entry and should be practiced often.

You can use this while charging in with a forward lever like the dive entry. You also can duck and then move in to get under the punches. Ideally, your elbows hit the attacker's chest and your head is underneath the attacker's chin. You can grab a body lock, rise up to a head butt or go directly for a takedown. You also can use this position if you have to run through a line of multiple attackers. The ram's horn entry is simple and effective — that is good silat!

1

2

3

4

Jarlo Ilano is ready to fire a barrage of strikes (1). Burton Richardson charges in a forward-lever position with the ram's horn entry (2) to smother the blows (3) and set up a strong head butt (4).

THAI COVER

This is an arm configuration that is used extensively in *muay Thai* kickboxing. In the sport, combatants generally use this to ward off punches while staying at a range to return kicks or knees. In the silat origins, it would also be used to enter deep on an adversary to attempt a takedown.

Put your lead hand behind your head and bring your forearm in snug against your ear. If your forearm is too high, there will be space for a closed fist to get through and hit you hard. Keep your hand low below the base of your skull and the cover tight. Be sure that your elbow does not point outward but instead is in front of your face. This closes the line for straight punches.

Extend your other arm with your palm open and fingers up to avoid getting them sprained. The lead side is similar to a one-armed ram's horn, and the other side is similar to a one-armed dive. Together, they make a strong structure for keeping punches and elbows off your head as you move in to take control of the fight.

The great benefit of this entry structure is that if you don't quite make it all the way in on the first movement, you are still covered quite well. You can throw kicks and make adjustments while deflecting punches until you can get to your preferred range. It works great in the incredibly rigorous world of muay Thai, and it can work for you in a self-defense situation.

1

2

3

Israel Cruz swings (1). Burton Richardson uses the Thai cover to block the punch while using his right hand to keep enough distance (2) to set up a strong knee strike (3).

FULL COVER (THE HELMET)

This is a universal block I developed in the 1990s that works against almost any striking attack at the head. It combines the Thai cover with the concept of bracing from silat. Bracing occurs when a blocking arm is reinforced by pushing on it with the other hand. This makes the block much stronger and more resistant to heavy blows. Building on the Thai cover, which has proved effective for centuries, the arm next to the head is strengthened because instead of extending the other arm, you use it to cover your face while bracing the covering arm. The result is that your head is protected from most strikes without having to make many adjustments.

The full cover blocks the jab, cross, rear hook, overhand and rear elbow, as well as attacks with impact weapons such as sticks, rocks and bottles. If a lead hook comes in to the open side of your face, just rotate slightly in the direction of the punch to block it. This cover has proved so effective that many groups have adopted it. It was given the nickname "the helmet" because it is like putting on a helmet to protect your head.

Note that the inside of the wrist of the supporting arm presses against your lead forearm to reinforce it. The supporting hand is open to help catch whatever is coming in, and the rear elbow is down to keep the uppercut line as small as possible. Look underneath your rear forearm as you charge forward.

As with all entries, you want to burst forward to cut into the assailant's attack. If you stay where you are, you will be hit with the full force of the strike. Moving in will smother the blow.

As you enter, you can drive your rear elbow or forearm into the aggressor's face. This further interrupts the attack and may hurt the aggressor.

Because it blocks so many strikes with little adjustment to the incoming blow, this cover is ideal for low-light situations in which you can't see exactly what is coming. And it requires very little timing because you just put on your "helmet" and charge forward. It is a great way to move into close quarters where you can maximize your silat skill.

1

2

Front view of the helmet (1). Side view of the helmet (2).

FLOWER

This entry is called the flower because of the corresponding dance movement. In the dance, the hands start together, travel upward and bloom open in opposite directions. For fighting, the hands move apart as one hand blocks and the other hits, checks or sometimes blocks, like against a two-hand push.

If a right swing comes in, the left arm comes up and toward the incoming arm. The forearm torques outward just as contact is made to add extra velocity to the blocking surface. That extra torque makes a notice-

The flower movement is often seen in Southeast Asian dances.

able difference in the power generated, meaning that you don't only stop an incoming blow but possibly inflict significant pain and damage to the aggressor's arm. This is why the hands and forearms in the dances often rotate and torque. It looks beautiful, but it is also quite applicable if you understand the movement and have practiced well.

As the blocking arm is extending outward, the other hand is exploding forward, usually toward the face. "Hand" is preferred to "fist" in that sentence because it affords a variety of tools that you can use with the same motion. You can punch with a closed fist, strike with an open hand, gouge at the eyes or use any other hand configuration you prefer. The idea of the flower is that you hit while you block before the attacker has a chance to throw a second strike.

You also can use interceptive timing with the flower. If you perceive the aggressor is preparing to attack, like in rearing back a fist before throwing a haymaker, you can hit first with the flower entry, keeping your blocking hand there in case the attacker's blow follows through.

The flower entry is very powerful and quite surprising to an assailant. Practice it well because you may be able to use the flower entry to end a fight before it even gets going.

This is the flower motion in action. Burton Richardson is in a ready position against an aggressor (1). When Jarlo Ilano swings, Richardson uses the flower entry to block and strike with an open palm simultaneously (2).

SLAP AND STRIKE

In many styles of silat, this is the preferred entry when dealing with a straight punch. Just like the flower is an efficient, aggressive entry against a swing, the slap and strike allows you to simultaneously block with one hand and hit with the other against a straight-line attack, be it a jab, cross, push or grab. Instead of hitting, if you choose, you also can check the aggressor's nonstriking hand.

When parrying on the outside, your striking hand can take two basic pathways: Because the incoming punch is straight, you can parry downward and strike over your arm, or you can parry slightly to the side and punch inside the attacker's arm. The method you use depends mainly on your positioning when the attack occurs. If you just want to control the aggressor as you enter, you can parry and check the other arm before it can fire and then you can secure a clinch position.

Slap-and-strike entries take more skill because you must first read that a straight punch is coming and then employ impeccable timing to step in and slap that full-speed, full-power punch out of the air. And you must step the correct distance to be able to strike at the same time. This is easy to do in practice when someone is feeding you punches at half speed, but it is considerably more difficult to apply when someone is trying to take your head off.

This entry can be applied often in high-intensity boxing/MMA sparring against experienced fighters because it is difficult for them to counter when it is timed correctly. Many advanced students can use this in heavy sparring, as well. Just remember that in a real fight, in which you may not be ready, simpler entries such as the dive and the covers have fewer moving parts and therefore have less chance of breaking down under pressure. But if you train well, you will be able to develop the skill to intercept a straight punch with the highly efficient slap-and-strike entry.

1

2

Burton Richardson is in the ready position (1). Israel Cruz fires a jab, but Richardson uses the slap-and-strike entry to block the punch while delivering a straight punch of his own (2). To acquire the timing necessary to pull this off, students must do a lot of sparring.

DOUBLE TRAP

This is a very simple entry used against someone who has his hands up in a boxing posture. Move in and jerk both the adversary's wrists down to open him up to a head butt, elbow, slap to the groin or takedown. It is suggested that you slip your head outside the aggressor's arms as you make the entry — in case he punches as you step forward. Taught by *tuhon* Dan Inosanto since at least 1980, this technique has recently started appearing in UFC fights. It's usually followed with an elbow. The double trap is a great way to enter with firepower.

1

2

3

Burton Richardson is in the ready position (1). Because Scott Ishihara's hands are up in a fighting stance, Richardson uses the female triangle footwork to move closer while getting his head off the line of Ishihara's punches (2). Getting his head out of the way of the aggressor's strikes is critical and allows Richardson to safely apply the double-trap entry, followed immediately with a strong elbow (3).

THREE-COUNT

This aggressive entry can be used from outside or inside the punching arm, against straight or curved punches. The key here is ferocious commitment to the entry. You must overwhelm the attacker with speed and forward pressure.

The movement is basically the same as that used in many double-sword or double-stick stroking patterns. If parrying a left straight punch from the outside, your right hand parries across, followed immediately by your left hand, which comes up from under your right arm. These first two movements are used to blast the punching arm aside, leaving an opening for the right hand to attack. The movement is done in an extremely fast and powerful rhythm. You can't "patty cake" the entry because you will get blasted by the attacker's second punch. This entry needs to be done with utter domination.

The first two movements blast the incoming arm to the side, but the three-count entry works even better when that second hand is driving in toward the attacker's face. Think of how fast a jab-cross comes in. If you wait until the third beat of your entry to attack, you may be eating that cross. You want to hit on that second motion to at least disrupt his balance so he can't fire a good second attack. The third movement, which can be a backhand or a forehand, continues the counter-assault and sets the aggressor up for your following moves.

To practice the three-count entry, Inosanto would have students put on boxing gloves and have partners throw full-speed punches. At first, everyone was surprised that the entry wasn't as easy as expected. But after several sessions of this drill, the students improved dramatically and gained timing and attitude. Spar it and you will understand how you need to really take over and enter deep with the three-count to make it work. In true silat fashion, you must crash that line.

The three-count is particularly useful when an aggressor attacks from the side because regular parries and blocks do not work as well. The compound effect of the three-count entry is a great solution for rear attacks, too.

Burton Richardson is lucky to see that Jarlo Ilano is attacking from the rear (1). Richardson ducks his chin and uses his right-hand parry (2). His left follows immediately to also block the arm (3). These two motions happen within a fraction of a second. In this instance, Richardson opts to use his right elbow strike as the third motion of the three-count (4).

SCOOP AND STRIKE (OR CHECK)

Last but not least, this is a common silat technique for dealing with a straight punch, but it takes even more skill than the parry. Not only do you block the punch aside, but you also have to use a circular motion to redirect the fist that is hurtling toward your face with vicious intent. The scoop is easy to apply in practice because partners rarely punch all the way through to the target. They usually stop a few inches in front of your head, so parrying from the outside and redirecting the strike from the inside is simple. Everything works when there is no resistance. But when someone is really trying to hurt you, that's another story. When practicing, it is important to regularly don good headgear and be sure your partner is punching through the target.

If you master this entry, it works wonders. Not only do you block the strike, but also redirecting it creates openings in the attacker's defense. This is a go-to move in hard sparring because it can confuse skilled opponents.

The trick is to parry with your wrist from the top of his arm and immediately use your fingers to scoop from the inside of his arm, knocking his hand away from his body. You can strike at the same time with the other hand, or you can use it to check the attacker's rear punch. By checking the attacker's other hand, both his arms are momentarily out of position and you can land your strike without impedance.

Note that the parry entries are *much* easier to apply against a push or a grab because the incoming arm isn't so ballistic. Some will say that it is a waste of time to practice the parries, such as the slap and strike, three-count, and scoop and strike because they don't work against an aggressive attacker who is really trying to take your head off, especially in a surprise attack. The dive, ram's horn, Thai cover, full cover and even the flower are much easier to apply and should be prioritized in training. You should give precedence to working those gross-motor-skill entries and truly master them. But do not limit yourself as long as you have your basics down, having functionalized them by training against resisting partners. There are times when the parries are applicable, especially against skilled strikers. Work on the parries and scoops so you will have more options in a serious situation in which the lives of your loved ones are at stake.

Israel Cruz and Burton Richardson are squared off in punching range (1). Cruz rips out a jab. Richardson steps diagonally forward while scooping the punch with his rear hand (2). This gives him the distance to check Cruz's rear arm before it fires (3). Richardson delivers a shocking upward elbow strike (4).

DRIFT ATTACK (OFFENSIVE)

When the fight is at kickboxing range but the skilled attacker is not moving forward aggressively, you will have to force your entry. One way is to just strike in combination while charging forward into close range, but a skilled striker will easily avoid your entry. It is better to fake out the aggressor by changing the line of your attack as you enter. These "drift attacks" look like they are going toward one target, and as the adversary defends, the attack changes direction and drifts to the actual intended target. For *jeet kune do* followers, this is what Bruce Lee termed the "progressive indirect attack."

Probably the most commonly used drift attack in silat starts with a movement toward the head and drifts down to the groin. It involves stepping diagonally forward using the female triangle or lightning-bolt footwork while you initiate a strike toward the head. As the assailant reacts to the high attack, drift your hand down to slap or grab the groin and continue into a takedown. It is an extremely effective offensive entry that is used in sparring on a daily basis.

1

2

3

4

Here is a great offensive entry when you need to close the distance. Start with an overhand open-palm strike. Keeping the hand open makes it look bigger and more threatening so the opponent will react to it (1). Scott Ishihara's hands go up to defend the strike (2). Burton Richardson changes the trajectory of the blow downward (3). He attacks the unprotected groin (4).

CHAPTER SIX

TAKEDOWNS

Takedowns are extremely important in silat. The attitude of the silat fighter is to put the attacker on the ground as quickly as possible to take away many of his tools, put him in a vulnerable position and possibly injure him as he hits the ground. Remember that sports such as wrestling and judo limit the types of takedowns to ensure the safety of the combatants. The sports avoid manipulating the joints of the neck, back or knees to avoid crippling injuries. Throws that land the opponent in a dangerous position are also illegal. But silat is designed for use when your life or the lives of your loved ones are at stake. The most injurious throws are prioritized.

Let me emphasize here (and I will point out again later when detailing the more dangerous takedowns) that *you must be extremely careful when practicing these moves!* You can seriously injure your partner with these takedowns, even when training slowly. When practicing the most dangerous throws in sparring, it is best to just get into a position in which you could apply the takedown without following through with the actual finish. Safety first!

One word to keep in mind as you practice the individual takedowns is "flow." Sometimes, you go for a throw and you make it happen. Other times, you have to feel what the opponent is giving you. The opponent's counter to one takedown usually leaves an opening to another. You may start a head tilt and the opponent swings his left leg back and around for balance, but that gives you the back sweep. This is flow! Stay on the offense long enough with forward pressure and you will find a place to move into a heavy takedown.

There are so many silat throws and variations that we don't have nearly enough space in this book to cover all of them. We will prioritize those that are simplest to apply yet devastatingly impactful against a fully resisting opponent.

HEAD TILT

The *tarik kepala* (head tilt) is extremely simple and has worked on numerous occasions, including many times in all-out stick fights as well as in moderate-intensity sparring. One specific instance was a stick-fighting match in the Philippines against the then-world champion, which resulted in the match being stopped.

The head tilt is a must-have takedown for your arsenal. Silat students who are in law enforcement have used this technique successfully to take down suspects while retaining control without causing injury. One such student reports that he has used the head tilt at least 20 times on the streets of New York City to make arrests. Assuredly, this simple takedown works very well. But as with all the throws, the mechanics are very important for maximum efficiency.

The opponent must be in a somewhat upright position. (Another type of takedown would be more successful if the person is bent over.) The key in tarik kepala is to tilt the head to the rear, and when the back of the head (occipital) is oriented downward, push straight down, trying to drive the opponent's head into the ground. Don't just push the head backward because the opponent can walk back out of it. You want the opponent in a severe backbend with locked-up vertebrae. The neck and spine bind up and the aggressor experiences a very uncomfortable fall. Do this takedown slowly in practice and be very controlled with it in sparring. But in self-defense, apply it explosively.

Although not necessary, it helps to block the opponent's lower back to keep the person from walking away and out of the throw. Even better than blocking the opponent's lower back, you can slap the person's kidney and grab skin to move the hips forward.

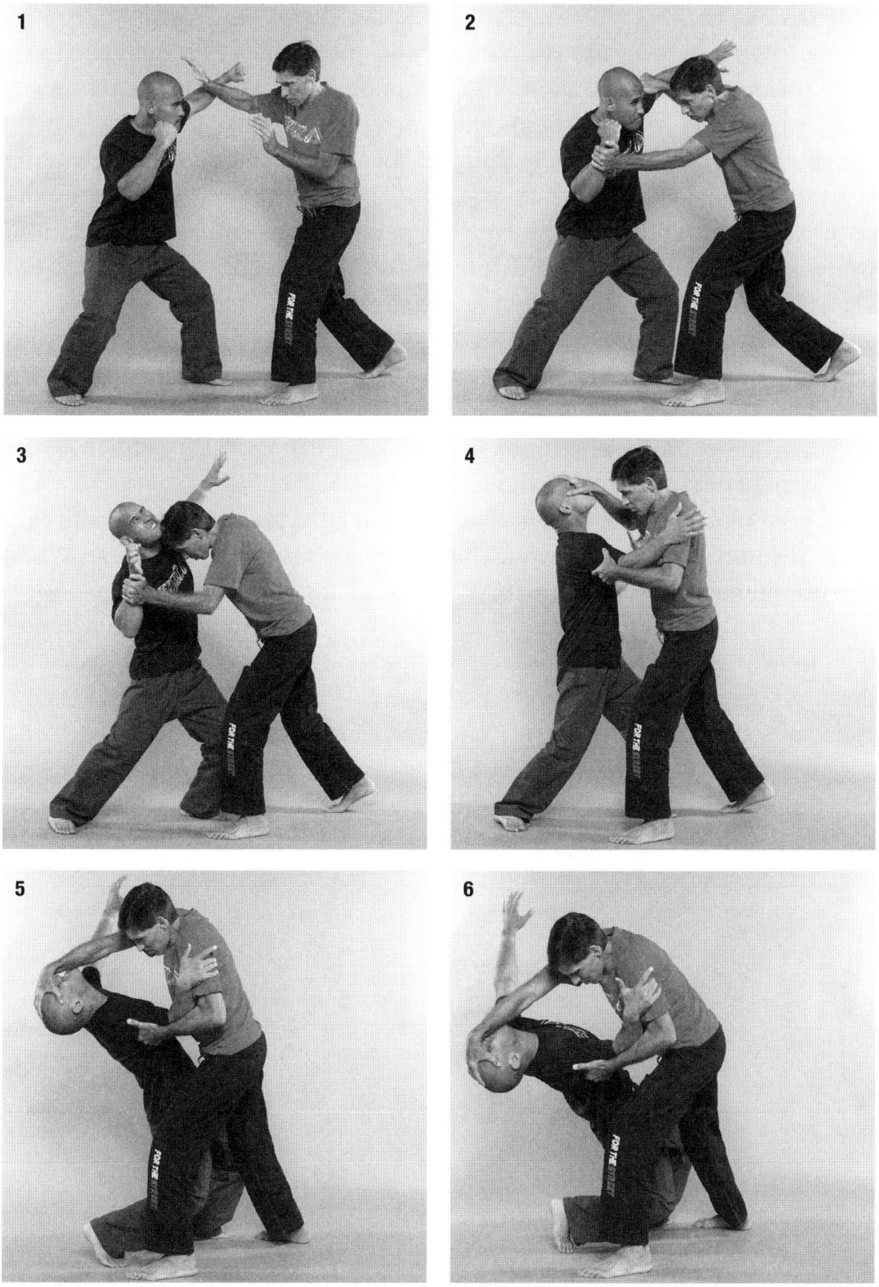

Jarlo Ilano fires a left hook (1). Burton Richardson uses the flower entry and checks Ilano's rear hand while grabbing behind his neck to set up a strong head butt (2-3). Richardson slams his right palm into Ilano's upper face (4), shoves backward (5) and then down for the head-tilt takedown (6).

THROAT GRAB

The *tenggorokan genggam* (throat grab) is another very simple takedown that works well. You simply grab the opponent's throat, block the lower back or leg, and drive through with forward pressure. The aggressor is bent backward and falls down. Simple. This is an easier takedown than the head tilt against a taller assailant, and you can better control the way the adversary lands and avoid injuring the person. In a self-defense situation, you will drive the assailant down hard into the ground.

Push upward and backward at the same time to get the aggressor up on his toes, and use forward pressure to follow through with the throw. If you just push straight back, it is much easier to counter. Another great benefit of the throat grab is that you can do it with relative safety in sparring, so you get more repetitions in while under the pressure of a resisting opponent. That ingrains the move.

This move can work even in sparring against experienced grapplers who are larger and stronger than you. The throat grab comes as a surprise. When the grappler straightens up to try to remove your hand, down he goes.

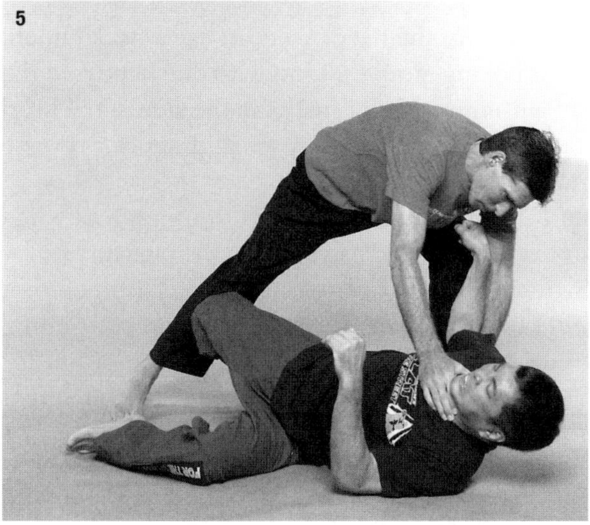

Burton Richardson uses the flower entry against Scott Ishihara's rear punch (1). Richardson ballistically strikes/grabs Ishihara's throat and drives him backward (2). Richardson continues the forward pressure while slapping Ishihara's lower back, which keeps Ishihara from stepping back to counter the pressure (3). Richardson finishes the takedown, slamming Ishihara to his back (4-5).

HEAD TWIST

Again, we are going for head control to secure a simple takedown. Note that the previous head-tilt and throat-grab takedowns are ways to control the head. That old saying, "where the head goes the body must follow," is certainly true. The head and neck of a very heavy opponent are vulnerable, even with a base that is difficult to upset.

The *puter kepala* (head twist) takedown requires more control of the head before applying, while the head tilt and throat grab are done more ballistically. But once you have control of the head with both hands, twisting in the correct direction with proper footwork makes for a spectacular takedown. When done at full speed, both the adversary's feet often come off the ground. A student who is very proficient with this takedown once used the neck-clinch version several times during hard sparring in his JKD Unlimited instructor test. He later became a police officer and uses it routinely against combative suspects who are much, much bigger and stronger than he is. He has gotten great results in the field with the head-twist takedown.

To secure the head, the opponent must be bent over a bit. You can force bending at the waist with groin strikes, a partial sweep or by pushing and pulling. Be sure your head control is very tight because you don't want the opponent slipping out.

There are several ways to secure the head. You can use a neck clinch, which is very popular in Thai boxing, grab the chin with one hand and the hair at the back of the head with the other, or just grab the side of the head with both your hands. You also can cross your arms and apply a reverse neck clinch.

To throw the aggressor to your left, step back with your left foot while keeping your upper body close to the head as you keep the pressure on by using your bodyweight. Swing your upper body back toward your left foot while twisting the opponent's head, right ear facing the ground and pulling the head diagonally down toward your left foot (extremely important for off-balancing). This provides maximum torque and keeps the opponent from being able to step forward for balance. A horizontal motion allows the aggressor to take a step and re-balance. A diagonal drive downward places the aggressor's weight on the right foot, anchoring it in place, and the person flies.

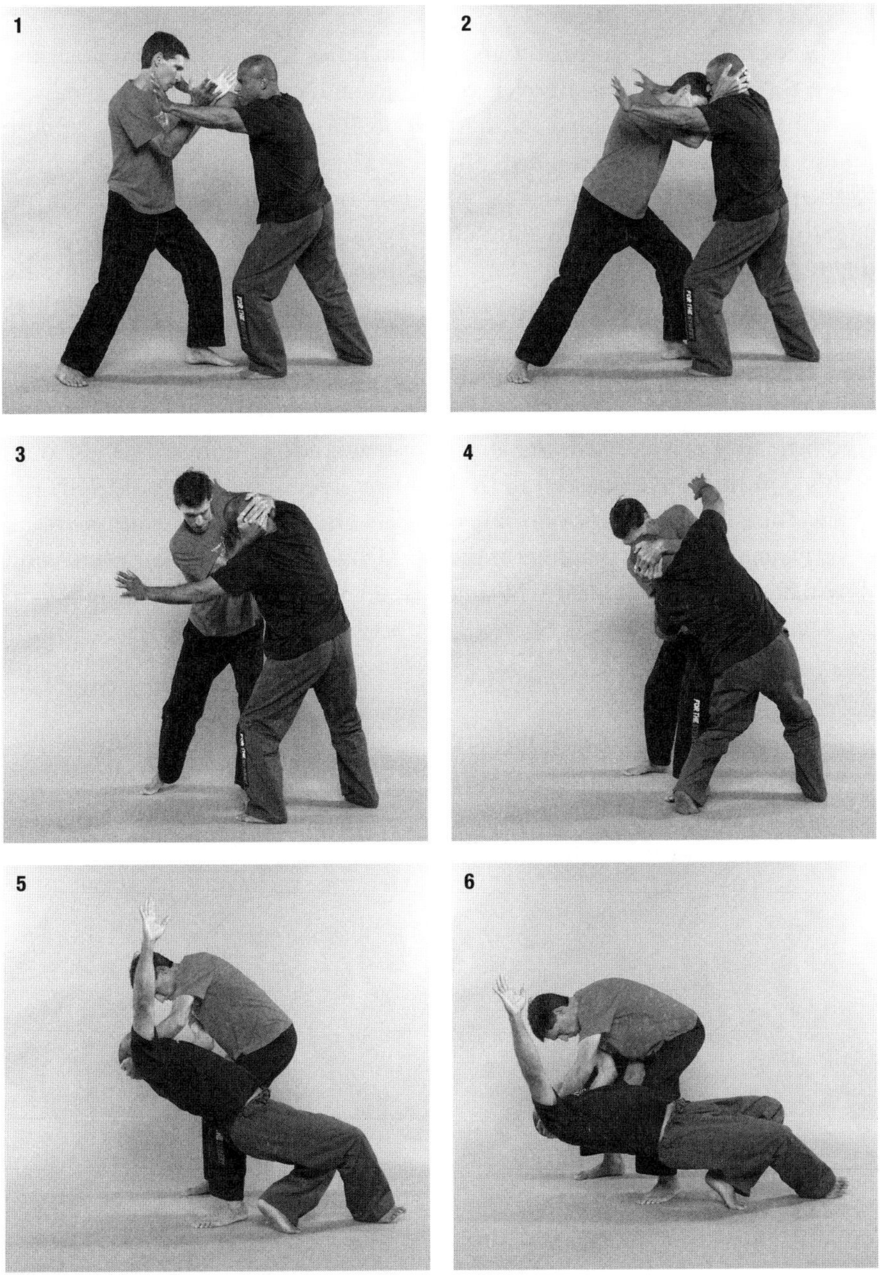

Burton Richardson uses the flower entry against Israel Cruz's two-hand shove (1). This gives Richardson inside position for the neck clinch and head butt (2). Richardson circles his right leg behind to use his bodyweight to twist Cruz's head and pull him off-balance (3-4). Richardson slams Cruz to the ground (5-6).

CHIN GRAB

This is a variation of the head twist, but it comes from a different position. When the opponent is bent over, you can reach over the back of the head to secure the *genggam dagu* (chin grab) position. Put downward pressure on the attacker with your chest, and keep your forearm high on the head so the person can't pull out of the position. Lean away and twist the head by pulling the chin up and around. Keep your forearm stuck to the back of the aggressor's head and travel away while stepping to the side, dropping your body and pulling in a tight circle. Push on the opponent's far shoulder to keep the person from spinning out of the takedown, and pull until the person is forced to fall onto his back.

Avoid doing this takedown in sparring because the move twists the vertebrae and can cause damage to people who do not have a very strong, highly conditioned neck. Get to the position, feel how you would start the throw, then let go and move on. It is highly effective. As an example of its effectiveness, a *jiu-jitsu* fighter at the Abu Dhabi Combat Club Submission Wrestling World Championship once used a variation of this takedown to put a great wrestler on his back.

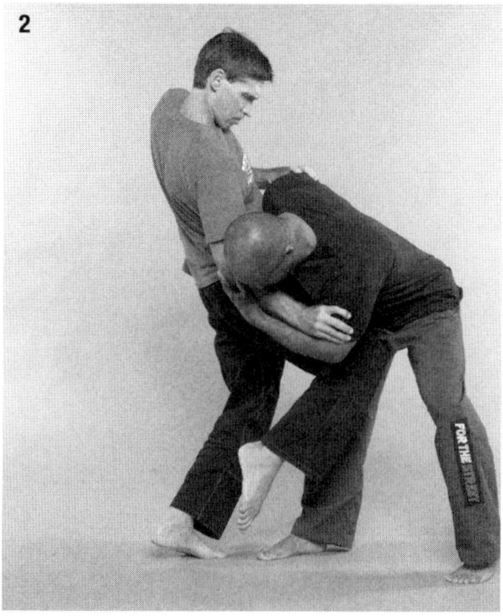

3

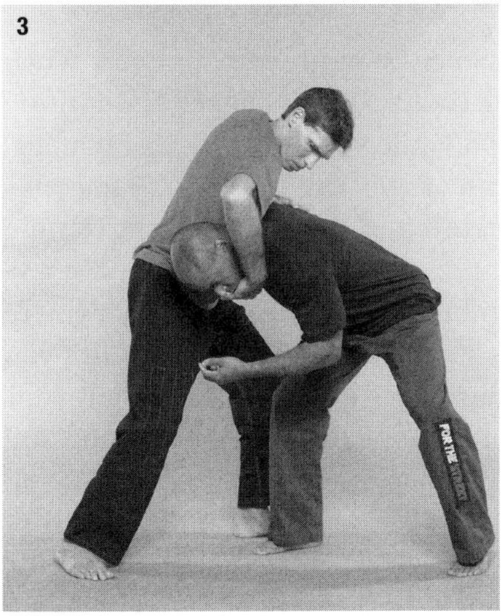

4

5

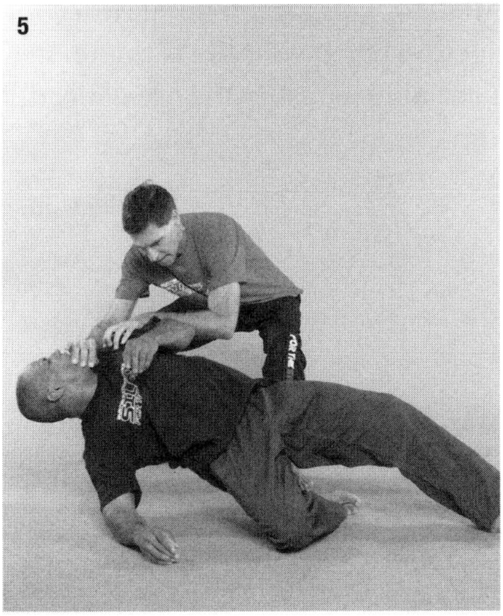

6

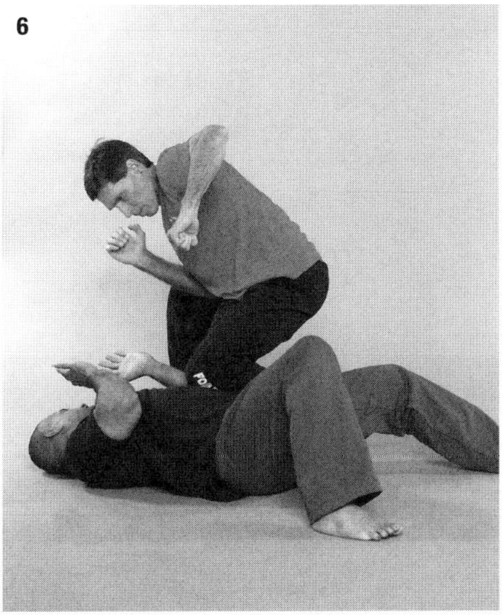

From the double-biceps grab position, Burton Richardson throws a knee to the groin, which bends Israel Cruz over (1-2). This gives Richardson the opportunity to reach over Cruz's head and grip his chin (3). Richardson steps back to the side and pulls Cruz's chin to twist his head while pushing on the shoulder to keep Cruz from spinning out (4). Richardson slams Cruz to the ground and takes the top position (5-6).

CRADLE THROW

This is a great example of a throw designed to injure the opponent when he hits the ground. The *angkat banting* (cradle throw) depends on lifting one of the opponent's legs off the ground while you are outside of that leg. Your other hand goes around the opponent's back at the waist. Bend your legs to get your hips under the opponent's and explode upward, leaning back while lifting.

It is important to lean back and pull the aggressor over you so you're using your legs to carry the weight. If you are bent over and try to lift, you will be relying on your lower back. Your lower back is weaker than your legs and you may injure yourself. So get underneath the opponent and pull the person back over your hips as you explode upward. Lift as high as you can and then drive the opponent down as hard as you can. You'll cause maximum damage by slamming the opponent down on the shoulder area. You'll knock the wind out of the opponent with a throw to the back. Be very aware that if you throw the attacker headfirst, you may kill him. That would mean severe moral and legal trouble for you, which could ruin your life. Only resort to that sort of extreme action when your life is threatened and you have no other choice. You must be able to justify the use of deadly force in a court of law.

1

2

3

4

5

6

Jarlo Ilano has Burton Richardson in the neck clinch. Richardson puts his forearm against Ilano's hip to slow down and lessen the power of the coming knee strike (1). As the knee arrives, Richardson sidesteps with his rear leg and tucks his body to avoid the blow (2). This puts Richardson in position to hook his right arm under Ilano's knee (3). Richardson brings his hips in close and wraps Ilano's waist with his left arm (4). Richardson explodes his hips inward and upward to lift Ilano, turn him and pile-drive him to the ground (5-6).

HEAD AND ARM TURN

The head and arm turn is a throw found in many martial arts. But it calls for a few words of warning. First, the move is often performed by grabbing the opponent's wrist, pushing down on the head and spinning the opponent to the ground. But doing this with a wrist grab is very difficult against someone who is fighting back. There is a lot of play in the arm because the elbow and shoulder joints can move and counter the throw. It is actually more secure when hooking under the elbow, but then you lose some leverage.

Second, you can't just grab someone who is resisting and turn the entire body. If the opponent stiffens up, you won't have the leverage to finish the throw. In training years ago, one of the strongest, most skillful students in the class got into the position while sparring against someone smaller and weaker. The smaller person just stiffened up and this powerful student could not complete the throw.

So what must you do to finish this throw? There are three elements that help tremendously. First, weaken the opponent through striking. If you hurt the attacker to the point of making him wobble, you can pull off almost any throw. Second, realize that this works very well when the opponent is bent over and rushing you. The opponent provides the momentum and won't have the base to stiffen up and resist the throw. In a sumo match in Japan, a fighter was observed pulling this off against a top *sumotori* who outweighed him by nearly 300 pounds. The huge fighter rushed in, and the small fighter pulled the opponent's head down, sidestepped while underhooking the elbow and tossed the sumotori off the platform. Brilliant.

The third enhancement is to use precise footwork to cut the angle. Instead of making the opponent fall with a 180-degree twist, turn the person's body 90 degrees while stepping behind to get to the other 90 degrees. The opponent goes down very easily when you time the step with the turn correctly. Totally resisting opponents are always surprised at how they suddenly feel like they have "fallen into a black hole." The details make all the difference.

1

2

3

4

5

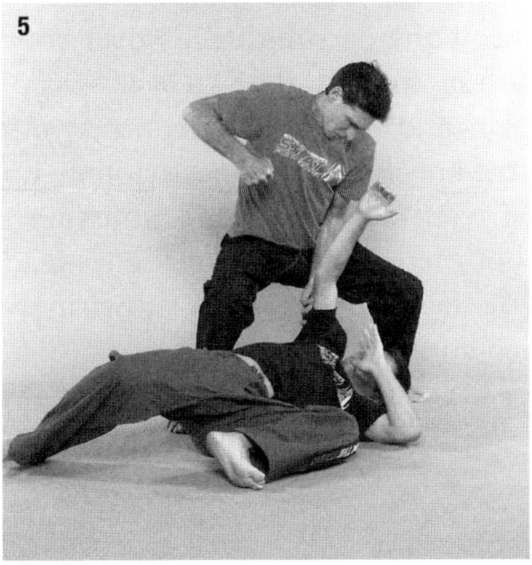

Burton Richardson has an underhook with neck control in the clinch (1). Scott Ishihara changes levels to shoot for a takedown (2). Richardson counters by moving back and pushing Ishihara's neck down (3). Circling to the side allows Richardson to pull Ishihara's arm farther (4). This results in the head-and-arm-turn takedown (5).

OUTSIDE BACK SWEEP

The *biset luar* (outside back sweep) is another type of takedown. Students must remember that the heavier the adversary, the more difficult it's going to be to sweep that leg. Off-balancing and timing are the keys.

To perform the back sweep, you need to off-balance the opponent and step past his lead leg while anchoring him over that leg (see "Be an Anchor" in the Functional-Silat Principles section) and retaining your own leverage position. You can just kick the leg out, which can work, but it is preferable to maximize the efficiency of the throw by using proper angulation.

Raise the opponent's head by pushing the chin or grabbing the throat and lifting. This gets the adversary up on his toes and into position for you to apply the back sweep. Ideally, you want the opponent's upright body turned so his shoulders are almost lined up toward you. You want most of the opponent's weight on the lead leg so sweeping out that leg will cause the opponent to fall down when you take it away. If most of it is on the rear leg, the opponent, to remain balanced, will simply lift up the foot you are sweeping. Pull down on the opponent's lead arm to anchor the opponent so he can't just step out of the position.

When you step through and behind your adversary's leg, you must maintain that forward lever. The most common mistake is to lean back and reach through with your sweeping leg without off-balancing the opponent. That puts you in position to be swept. If you can't step through maintaining your lever position, go back to hitting while you move to another takedown.

Another common error is maintaining the forward lever but collapsing your arms as you step. If you collapse your arms, you won't off-balance the aggressor.

Once in proper position, maintain your anchor, rotate your body and manipulate your adversary's head to throw the person directly over your thigh. You can often finish the throw without actually doing a back sweep, but kicking out the leg makes up for errors and any efforts to counter you.

You also can do a back sweep from the kneeling position as a follow-up if you are very close to getting a regular back sweep but can't quite finish it. Just switch your grip so you have both hands on the opponent's lead arm, anchor hard and pull the person over your thigh. It is a surprisingly quick and painful takedown when timed correctly.

1

2

3

4

5

6

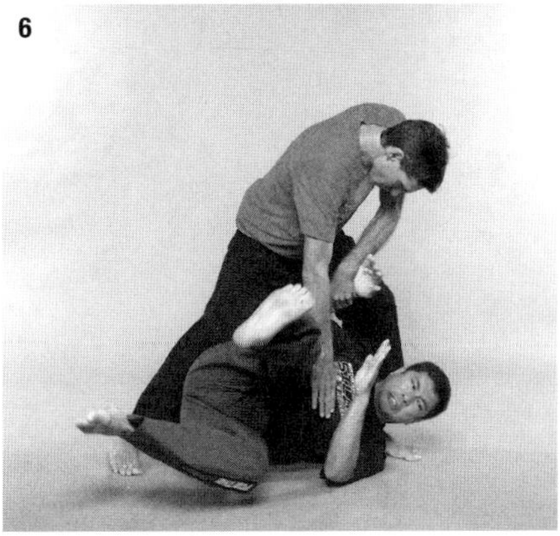

Scott Ishihara shoves Burton Richardson's shoulder. Richardson wipes it off and moves to the forward-lever position while securing Ishihara's biceps and throat (1-2). Making a way and maintaining the forward lever, Richardson steps deep behind Ishihara's lead leg while anchoring Ishihara's right arm to keep him from stepping back (3). Richardson turns and forces Ishihara over his leg (4). This drives Ishihara down for a hard fall (5-6).

INSIDE BACK SWEEP

The *biset dalem* (inside back sweep) is more difficult to finish because the attacker can bend forward to re-balance. This is why the inside back sweep is often used as a setup to off-balance an aggressor.

If you can get the proper momentum and angulation, you can finish the inside back sweep. The key is to move in and rock the opponent hard as you step inside the lead leg while maintaining a strong lever position. The strong entry is to get the aggressor's weight on the rear leg and make a way for your body and leg to enter. The opponent will probably push toward you to get weight back on the lead leg and re-balance. As the opponent's weight is transferring forward, back-sweep the leg and rotate your upper body to send him diagonally down toward your stationary foot.

This throw is often demonstrated from outside the opponent's outstretched arm, but in a real fight, an aggressor will not hold an arm out for you. It is much easier from head control, a bent arm lock, an underhook or an overhook.

Even if you can't throw the aggressor, the inside back sweep will get the person bent forward so you can fire a knee to the head or transition to another takedown.

1

2

3

4

5

6

Jarlo Ilano pulls Burton Richardson's shoulder to set up a sucker punch (1). Richardson uses a biceps stop to block the punch (2). Then he steps inside with his right leg with a forward lever while hooking his right arm under Ilano's left (3). Richardson turns and lifts Ilano's left arm while pulling Ilano's right inward (4). Richardson sweeps Ilano's left leg (5). He torques Ilano to the ground to finish the inside back-sweep throw (6).

BICYCLE STEP

The *sepeda langkah* (bicycle step) can be a throw in itself, but it is usually used as a quick way to get the opponent's leg to move and set up another throw.

Turn as if your going for the inside back sweep, but because you can't move the person to get to the proper position, point your toes and reach back as far as you can. The back of your thigh will touch the opponent's. Once your toes touch down, slam your heel to the ground to straighten your leg. It is important to get your thigh traveling slightly upward to uproot the opponent's foot, so bend forward as you do the bicycle step. This knee-straightening action will knock the person's leg back and his foot off the ground. With the adversary on one leg, you may be able to finish the throw to the ground with a torquing action. If that doesn't work, you can flow to other moves, such as a shin bind, a back sweep on the support leg or striking to the groin. The bicycle step is a very valuable move to affect a strong opponent's balance.

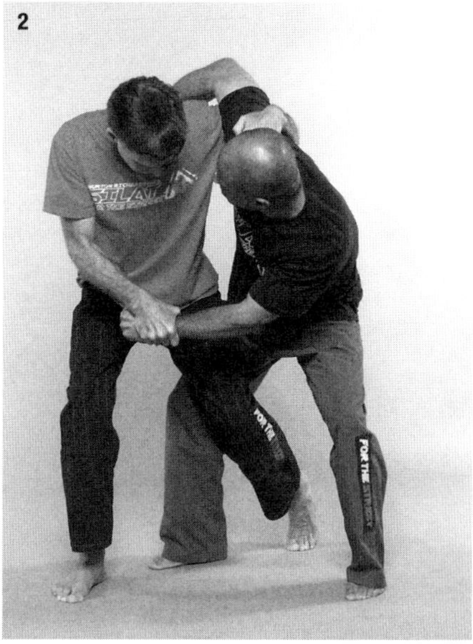

3

4

5

Burton Richardson tries for the inside back sweep, but Israel Cruz is too rooted and his leg won't budge (1). Keeping his thigh in contact with Cruz's leg, Richardson reaches his toes back as far as he can (2). Then he slams his heel to the ground while bending forward to pop Cruz's foot off the ground (3). With Cruz on one leg, Richardson can step behind Cruz's left leg and transition to a huge outside back-sweep throw (4-5).

OUTSIDE FOOT SWEEP

The *sapu luar* (outside foot sweep) is another takedown used many times in Dog Brothers fighting, tournaments and other full-resistance situations. Sweeping properly from the outside of the leg makes the opponent fall backward toward his weakest point, so it is more reliable than sweeping from the inside of the leg.

The keys to the foot sweep are timing, proper angulation on the sweep and accuracy.

- Timing. You can't do the sweep when an opponent's weight is all on the lead foot. It is too hard to move that leg unless the person is very light. Assuming the attacker is your weight or heavier, you have to move or coax the person into the proper position or recognize when the attacker is in a position to be swept.

1

2

3

4

5

6

Jarlo Ilano and Burton Richardson square off (1). When Ilano fires a foot jab to the midsection, Richardson scoops from the outside to catch the kick (2). He then pulls Ilano's leg back and downward to the side, causing Ilano to catch his balance in a wide stance (3). Richardson pushes Ilano's shoulder to keep him from moving his weight over his left foot (4). Lining himself up, Richardson applies the foot sweep (5-6).

- Proper Angulation. Just sweeping the leg in any direction is not going to give you good results. You need to sweep at the optimal angle to get optimal results. Visualize a baseline between the opponent's two feet and extrapolate it toward you. For the outside sweep, you want to take the opponent's foot/leg 30 degrees off that line in front of you. That will give you very good results. For the most efficient sweep, you want the opponent's upper body moving at 30 degrees off the line behind you. This splits the attacker's upper and lower body in two different directions. Down goes your adversary.

  A wide stance automatically makes it difficult to shift bodyweight. That kind of stance primes an opponent for a sweep. In this case, you don't need to manipulate the upper body. Sweeping at the precise 30-degree angle makes the sweep work very well.

  Note that the sweeping foot does not travel parallel to the ground. You come in low and sweep diagonally upward, which helps uproot the opponent's foot from the ground. There is also a slight torque of the foot to give a little extra oomph when contact is made to send the opponent's leg in the correct direction.

- Accuracy. If you hit the outside of the opponent's foot or ankle with your foot, you will end up with no sweep and a sore foot. Ideally, the arch of your foot should connect just below the bottom of the opponent's calf. Targeting a little below the midpoint of the lower leg maximizes your ability to get the foot up off the ground. The closer to the ground you do your sweep, the more power you will have to generate. The closer to the knee you sweep, the more likely that the adversary's knee will bend forward and you won't get the foot off the ground. The sweet spot is just below the calf.

Sweeps That Work

Put together the timing, angulation and accuracy and you have a takedown that drops skillful opponents. It takes a lot of dedicated, disciplined practice to develop the skill. I can tell you that when you pull off a sweep in a fight, all that work is well worth it. Here are two honest, personal examples (not bragging) of how this sweep can work.

- An accomplished *silat* instructor was visiting America, and after I took a lesson from him, he asked me if I wanted to do some sparring. (Yes, silat instructors from Indonesia do spar!) I of course said yes. He had chest protectors and gloves, which we donned. His particular style used a very wide stance, and his feet were lined up toward me. He threw a lot of quick kicks and punches, along with low, spinning back sweeps. I was able to apply the outside foot sweep on him several times because of his wide stance. But it worked so well because I was sweeping at that precise angle. The angle was the key detail that made the sweep effective. The lesson: Drill your sweeps precisely.

- I once used the outside foot sweep against a formidable opponent in a stick-fighting tournament. In that tournament, three disarms, three sweeps or a combination adding up to three meant an automatic win. I had already disarmed him twice, and one more disarm would result in a TKO, so he put his left foot forward to keep his right stick arm in the back and protect it from being disarmed again. We both moved in, crashed, and his left foot was in perfect position for a sweep. I hit the sweep and down he went. All those repetitions of sweeping during *jurus* and *langkahs* (one-person forms and footwork) and partner training had given me the proper angle and accuracy. Years of actual stick fighting had given me the ability to apply it at the correct time under the pressure of a real fight.

INSIDE FOOT SWEEP

The *sapu dalem* (inside foot sweep) can be used as a takedown if the angulation of the upper and lower bodies is just right. Keep in mind that it is much easier for the opponent to re-balance by bending forward at the waist and bracing against you or the ground. Also, be aware that if you are outside the opponent's lead arm when you line yourself up for the inside foot sweep, there's a clear pathway to your back, an opening that any grappler is going to exploit. So I suggest keeping your hands and body inside the adversary's lead arm when performing the inside foot sweep if you are at close range.

The angles are different from the outside foot sweep. For the outside sweep, the foot goes 30 degrees off the baseline while pulling the upper body 30 degrees in the opposite direction. For the inside sweep, the foot goes 30 degrees off the line, but the upper body, which must be at least slightly bent over, is pulled parallel to the line. This creates an efficient sweep.

Allow a little space between you and the attacker to perform this sweep. If you are body to body, you are too close to get the arch of your foot to the top of the opponent's Achilles tendon. (A knee bump works well here.) If the opponent is pushing away from the clinch or if you strike and make the person step back, you will have the proper distance for the sweep.

Use the inside sweep mainly as a setup for striking, head grabbing, moving to the back or transitioning to another takedown. If you rely on it solely as a takedown, you will find that the opponent can usually recover very quickly. Silat fighters always think of attacking in combination, so you should think of this sweep as the first move in a chain of techniques.

1

2

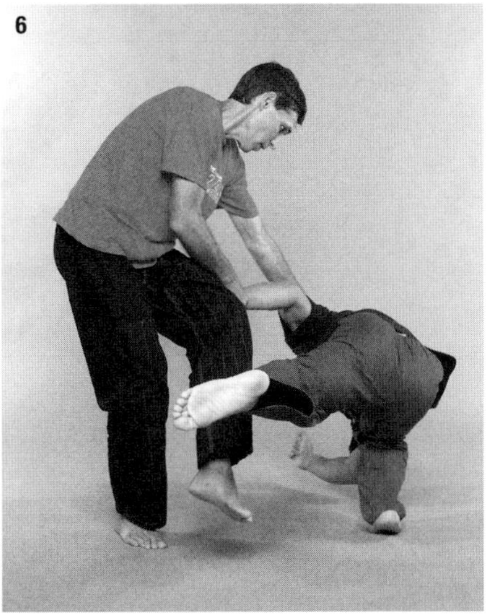

Burton Richardson and Jarlo Ilano square off (1). Ilano throws a right Thai kick, which Richardson stops with a push kick to the thigh (2). As Ilano recovers, Richardson steps in aggressively with a palm strike to the face while grabbing his left wrist (3-4). With his left foot inside Ilano's left, Richardson grabs Ilano's neck and pulls at the proper angle while sweeping him to the ground (5-6).

BEAR HUG

The *peluk* (bear hug) takedown is often seen in videos of Indonesian village matches. Slide both your arms under those of the attacker. You have two basic positions: either hold very high under his armpits or grab low around his lower back. If you grab high, you limit his ability to use his arms to counter or strike, and with his weight up on his toes, you can hook a leg to trip the attacker. If you grip low on his torso, you can step in, lift and throw. Maintain a strong posture so you lift with your legs, not your lower back.

Forward pressure is very important in getting your adversary backpedaling as you do the trip. If he is able to plant his feet, that sets him up for the lift and throw.

3

4

5

6

Burton Richardson uses the ram's horn entry against Jarlo Ilano's aggressive barrage of strikes (1-2). This puts Richardson in position to grab Ilano's body (3). He drives his hips in to lift Ilano (4). Richardson turns Ilano and slams him on his back (5-6).

ELBOW COMPRESSION

Here is a silat throw that is often used in muay Thai fights. The idea in *kenjit siko* (elbow compression) is to step behind the opponent's lead leg while driving your arm across the chest so that you can push the person back and over your thigh.

If the adversary's left leg is forward, twist your stance, lean forward into a strong lever position and drive your right arm across the chest at an angle so you bend the person backward. Strive to drive the opponent's upper body toward the point of that rear triangle. With your right leg, step in deep behind the left leg and slam your thigh into the opponent's thigh. If your adversary re-balances, maintain your forward lever and compress your elbow into the chest while twisting toward the rear to drive the person over your thigh. The goal is to make the opponent's head fall next to your rear foot. The fall is awkward and the impact is very hard, so be very careful when doing this in practice.

An off-balanced aggressor who doesn't fall is still wide open for strikes to the groin. So either way, you are in a position of advantage.

3

4

5

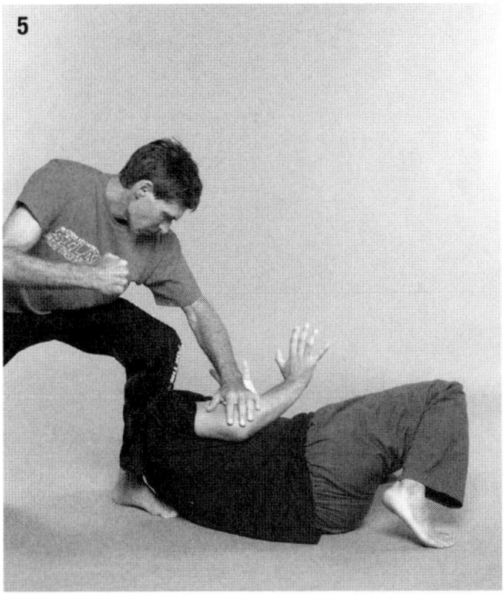

Burton Richardson and Scott Ishihara are in the ready position (1). Richardson catches Ishihara's foot jab and pulls to off-balance him (2). Richardson steps in deep in a side lever with his arm angled across Ishihara's chest (3). Then Richardson turns and compresses his elbow to throw Ishihara over his thigh (4). The result is a very hard landing (5).

DOUBLE-LEG LIFT

The position for the *angkat kaki* (double-leg lift) is the same as for the elbow-compression throw. Your lead arm is in front of the attacker's chest; your lead leg is behind the attacker's lead leg. But instead of driving the opponent backward, squat down and grasp and lift both the opponent's legs.

You must be in a strong side-lever position before you grab the legs. This will ensure that you are pushing the opponent over your thigh and not lifting with your lower back. As you squat and bend over to grab the adversary's legs, rock your hips forward to tilt the person rearward over your thigh. Lift explosively, turn and dump the opponent hard. If you are grabbed, you will go to the ground with the opponent, but you will land hard on top and be in a favorable position, past the opponent's guard.

This looks like a power move, but because of your deep position, you actually first pull the opponent back over your thigh before lifting. This means that most of the weight actually rests on your thigh. Students are always surprised that they can lift much heavier partners with the double-leg lift. Using your thigh as a fulcrum gives you the leverage to topple a big opponent. It is also a great answer to a high rear bear hug.

1

2

3

4

5

6

Israel Cruz has a high rear bear hug. Burton Richardson tries to open the grip but can't (1). Because the lock is high, Richardson's hips are free to move. He steps around Cruz's right leg (2), plants his foot deep to block Cruz's legs and uses the side lever to drive Cruz's upper body back while grabbing under both legs (3). Because of the lever position, Richardson can push Cruz back over his leg (4), which makes it very easy to lift him high (5). Richardson slams Cruz to the ground and lands with all his weight on Cruz's chest, compounding the force of the impact (6).

KNEE COMPRESSION

Controlled, safe sparring is essential for acquiring the necessary timing, perception and distance to pull off your techniques. Some teachers tell students that their style is "too deadly to spar," but you can always spar punches, kicks, elbows, knees, groin strikes, throat grabs and most takedowns. However, some techniques *are* too dangerous to use in sparring, and the *kenjit kaki* (knee compression) is one of them. *Do not use this technique in sparring because you will likely tear the ligaments in your partner's knee!* In addition, be *very careful* when practicing this with a cooperative partner. If you push a little too far, the knee may go. When the knee compression was first introduced to the American public in the late 1980s, many people suffered serious knee injuries from practicing this takedown, and that was without resistance. So just get into position and don't even move your partner's knee.

The technique is based on collapsing the leg by driving your foot through the side of the knee. The knee does not bend in that direction, so ligaments rip. The sound that knee ligaments make when they tear is something no one wants to hear in practice.

It is best to have the opponent's bodyweight over the leg so the foot doesn't slide out and there is a further collapsing and tearing effect during the fall. It is easiest to tilt the attacker's head over the lead leg while turning to face that leg. Bring your rear foot up to the outside above the knee, and stomp diagonally down through the side of the knee while driving the person's head straight down toward the ankle. Stomping at an angle (instead of horizontally) aids in anchoring the foot. As the knee collapses sideways, the attacker's bodyweight will fall straight down, adding to the snapping pressure on the ligaments. It is a decisive way to take out a vicious attacker.

To have it at your disposal without sparring, you will need to do thousands of dry-run repetitions, then get close to the position during your resistance sessions. Just don't follow through! With enough proper practice, you will be able to apply it under pressure to the great detriment any criminal who assaults you.

1

2

3

4

5

Burton Richardson is tied up with Jarlo Ilano, grabbing his neck and triceps (1). Richardson fires a snap kick to the groin (2). Ilano somehow survives and brings his right leg forward in front to protect his groin (3). With his right foot now forward, Richardson uses his right hand to turn and tilt Ilano's head to the side while preparing to stomp diagonally down for the knee compression (4). Tilting Ilano's upper body over his leg puts more weight driving down on the knee as it collapses, adding to the shearing force on the ligaments (5).

CROSS-ARM-LOCK THROW

Some readers may think this technique is in the realm of fantasy until they start getting this throw consistently in sparring. As always, the keys to actually applying a technique you have memorized are recognition and timing, acquired through lots of training with a resisting partner.

To do the throw, get the adversary's arms crossed at the elbows. Push on the vertical arm while pulling on the horizontal arm to keep it straight. Turn in the direction of the throw to maximize your leverage. As you continue to push and pull, you will cause a hyperextension of the elbow, which coaxes the opponent to fall. It isn't a primary move at all, but it is really fun when you can pull this one off.

1

2

3

4

5

6

Israel Cruz grabs Burton Richardson's neck with his right hand (1). Richardson turns his shoulder into the arm (a wrestling counter to the single neck grab) while using the kali-silat two on one to push Cruz's arm away (2). Richardson tries to use the opening to move to the back, but Cruz blocks the transition by putting his left forearm across Richardson's throat (3). Richardson retains his grip on the wrist with his right hand and brings his left hand inside Cruz's blocking arm (4). He grabs Cruz's left wrist, turns and achieves the cross-arm-lock position (5). Richardson turns hard while pulling on Cruz's left arm and pushing on his right to force Cruz to fall from the pressure of the arm lock (6).

Thoughts on a Clinch Position

If you get to the *silat* two on one (a clinch position described in the next chapter), you can push the attacker's arm toward his chest and move to his back. I pulled this off for a few weeks while sparring against a partner who is good in the clinch. Then my partner discovered a counter — he used the forearm of his free hand to brace across my throat, creating a barrier until he could free his arm from my grip. (This counter is used against the arm drag in Greco-Roman wrestling.)

One day, as I tried the move and my partner countered, my left hand released the grip on the opponent's triceps, grabbed the wrist of his blocking arm and torqued his arms into the cross-arm-lock throw. It wasn't done consciously, but years of working on the position with a cooperative partner had burned a pathway into my subconscious. When the position presented itself, my body did the move. I was shocked!

KICK CATCHES

Catching kicks is an important strategy in silat. When a kick comes in, you don't just want to block it; you want to capture it and use the opportunity to put your attacker at a distinct disadvantage.

Once you catch a kick, your attacker is on one leg and vulnerable, so immediately strike, do a takedown or strike to set up the takedown. Since one leg is up in the air, the primary striking follow-up is to kick or knee repeatedly to the groin, which usually results in the aggressor falling to the ground. You also can kick the knee of the support leg to damage it and make the attacker fall.

But striking does take a few seconds, which is a long time when there is more than one assailant. The takedown happens in a fraction of a second, so you may choose to throw immediately. The two most common takedowns from a kick catch are to kick out the attacker's support leg or raise the leg high and run forward, causing the attacker to crash to the ground. If you choose to kick the support leg out, know that hitting the back of the support leg causes a backward fall. Kicking the leg out from behind is the preferred move because the attacker will take a hard backward fall and is more vulnerable to quick striking follow-ups. Kicking the front of the support leg causes a facedown landing, which is an easier fall but exposes the person's back to you.

Lifting and running for the takedown is especially useful against multiple opponents because you can create distance from the other attacker(s) and possibly head toward an escape route. Use your environment when lifting and running. Slam the attacker into a wall, car or other hard object to make the fall even more severe.

When you catch a kick, realize that you are not out of danger. Be aware that the attacker could draw a weapon, start hitting you or lean forward to clinch you before you complete the takedown. Many silat stylists will counter the kick catch by leaping and throwing a head kick with their free leg. Use the kick catch immediately before the aggressor can re-balance and continue the assault.

As in fighting or in life, when an opportunity arises, you must take advantage of it immediately because it won't be there long. Catch that kick and use it to win the fight.

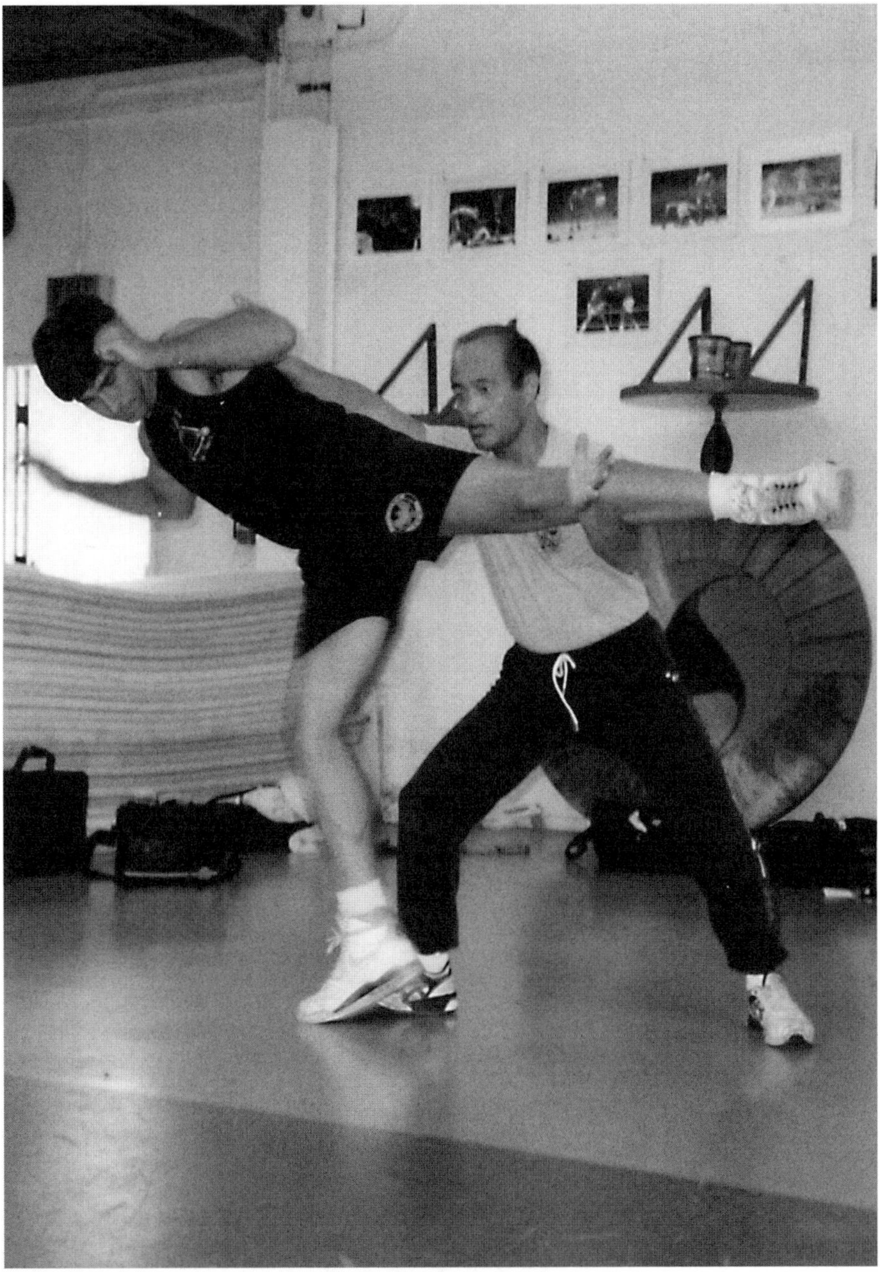

Dan Inosanto catches Burton Richardson's kick.

Catch a midline round kick by wrapping the arm over the leg.

Catch a high round kick by wrapping the arm under the leg.

Catch a straight kick by moving back and capturing the foot with both hands.

Shelve a side kick by sidestepping and bringing the outside arm up underneath the kicking leg.

LOW TAKEDOWNS — TIGER STYLE

Most styles of silat incorporate takedowns from the ground, but the system most famous for this tactic is the harimau (tiger) style from Sumatra. They often begin in a low position and leap at the opponent like a tiger pouncing on prey.

In a street situation in the Western world, you may not want to drop to the ground when an attacker approaches. It can work as a surprise attack, but in the street, try to avoid being under an aggressor. But in case you do end up on the ground, having a varied arsenal at your disposal will come in handy. Here are a few takedowns that work well from the low position against a standing attacker.

Knee-Lever Sweep

This is quite simple. You lie on your side and hook your bottom foot behind the Achilles tendon of the attacker's lead leg and pull as you perform a strong side kick with the top foot to the attacker's knee to hyperextend it. This works very well as long as the attacker's knee is not bent forward in a strong stance toward you because you won't be able to hyperextend the knee for the takedown.

An important detail is to face the attacker when you attempt this takedown. If the person's left foot is forward, lie on your left side to apply the knee lever. If you lie on your right side to do the takedown but miss, your back is exposed and the attacker may end up behind you.

3

4

5

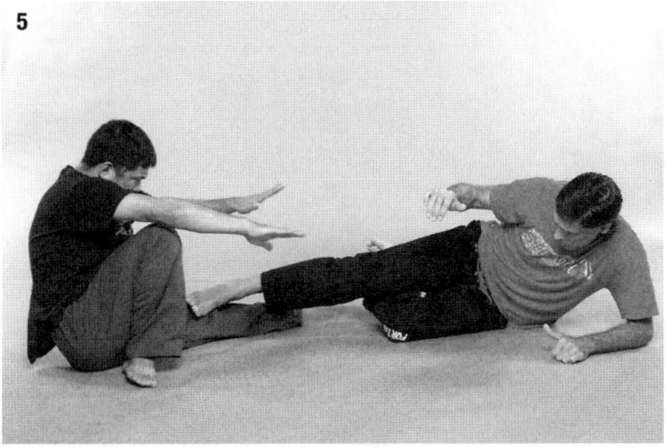

Burton Richardson has ended up on his back with Scott Ishihara standing over him (1). Richardson fires a front kick to the groin (2). This gives Richardson time to hook his bottom foot around the outside of Ishihara's lead foot while driving a hard side kick to Ishihara's knee (3). Ishihara's knee is hyperextended and he falls (4). From here, Richardson can escape or get on top to finish (5).

Knee Pull

This sweep was originally done with a *karambit* or similar hook knife in the hand. The karambit makes the move extremely effective. But it can work with empty hands, as well. As with any technique that applies force to the inside or outside of the knee, please use extreme caution when practicing. You risk tearing a partner's ACL if you practice this move carelessly — it's been known to happen.

Whether dropping from standing or starting from the ground, lay the side of your leg on the ground and place your foot against the side of the attacker's lead foot. This keeps the opponent's foot from sliding away or twisting to counter the takedown. Grip inside the knee with your hand and dig your fingers into the flesh behind the knee. Lean your upper body to the side and pull the knee outward and to the ground. For self-defense, this should be done with explosive intent. From here, you can kick to the groin or stand up.

Use caution: The opponent can counter your takedown and may move to your back by rotating the knee outward in the direction of the throw. Keep this in mind if you choose to attempt the knee-pull takedown.

1

2

3

4

5

In a confrontation, Burton Richardson adjusts his posture to draw the high punch from Israel Cruz (1). As Cruz fires, Richardson drops into the knee-pull position (2). He slams his left foot outside of Cruz's right and grabs deep inside the knee (3). Richardson continues to the side, using all his bodyweight to pull the knee and finish the takedown (4-5).

Low Ankle Dive

This is a fully committed move common to harimau. Using your entire bodyweight, you dive very low at the attacker's leg for the takedown. This is a good tactic to use against an aggressor who is too dangerous to stand with.

If you are standing, first drop down to a squat. If you are already down, prime yourself in a position where you can launch your body explosively at the opponent, like a tiger leaping out of the bushes. Dive at the inside of the attacker's leg with your head next to the shin and grasp the heel with your hands as you drive your shoulder into the inner side of the leg, just above the ankle. The ankle will buckle and this forces the attacker to the ground. Under the proper circumstances, this is a surprising and very effective move.

A great example of this takedown in combat sports occurred when Randy Couture fought former heavyweight boxing champ James Toney in the UFC. Couture has good striking, but Toney's incredible knockout power was such a threat that Couture chose to take the boxer down. Which takedown did he use? The wrestling version of the low ankle dive — and it worked perfectly. In the right circumstances, the low ankle dive could be your safest move.

1

2

3

4

If you are already on the ground — at the beach or in a park, for example — you can use this type of bait and takedown. Burton Richardson is in a side-sitting harimau position with his posture up to draw a head punch. Jarlo Ilano takes the bait and Richardson ducks by leaning to the side (2). He drives his shoulder into the inside of Ilano's ankle while wrapping up the foot with his hands (3). Richardson continues to drive forward to finish the low ankle-dive takedown (4).

FLOWING FROM TAKEDOWN TO TAKEDOWN

Here are a few examples of flowing from takedown to takedown. Remember that forward pressure is very important to keep the adversary on the defense while maintaining close range so you can strike and throw. Overwhelm your opponent with pressure!

Head-and-Arm-Turn Throw to Elbow Compression

1

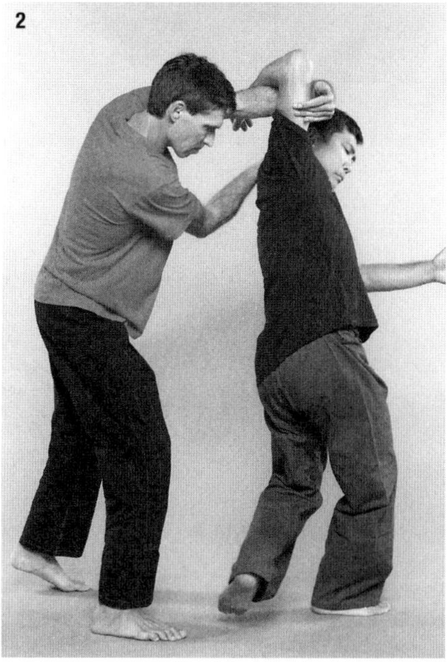
2

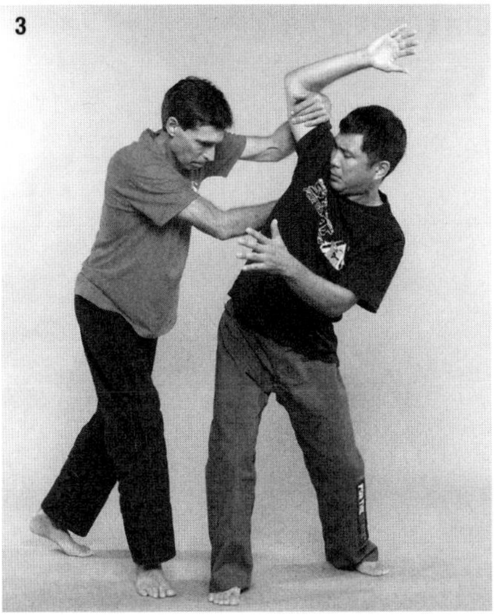

Burton Richardson is attempting a head-and-arm-turn throw against attacker Scott Ishihara, who goes with the movement and turns out of it (1-3). This gives Richardson the opportunity to step deep with a side lever while sliding his arm across the attacker's chest and delivering a powerful groin slap (4-5). Richardson can finish with the elbow-compression takedown (6).

Inside Foot Sweep to Head-and-Arm-Turn Throw

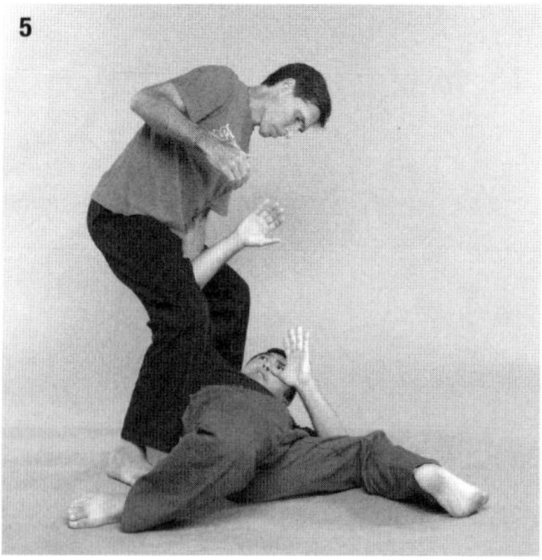

When Burton Richardson is applying the inside foot sweep (1), attacker Scott Ishihara bends over and shifts his weight to catch his balance (2). But this leaves Richardson in position to push Ishihara's head down while hooking under his arm to apply the head-and-arm-turn takedown (3-5).

Knee Pull to Arm Weave

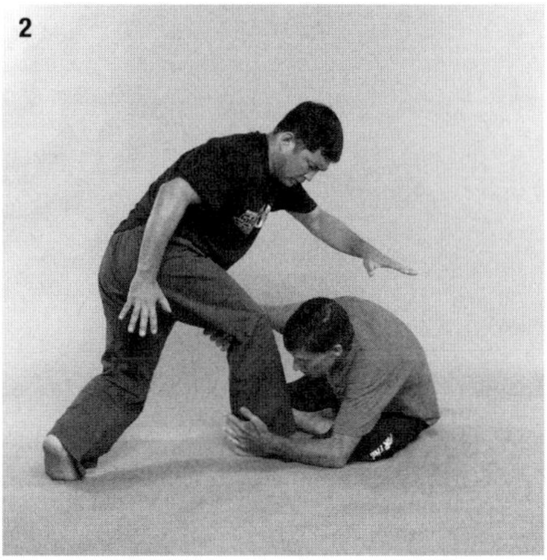

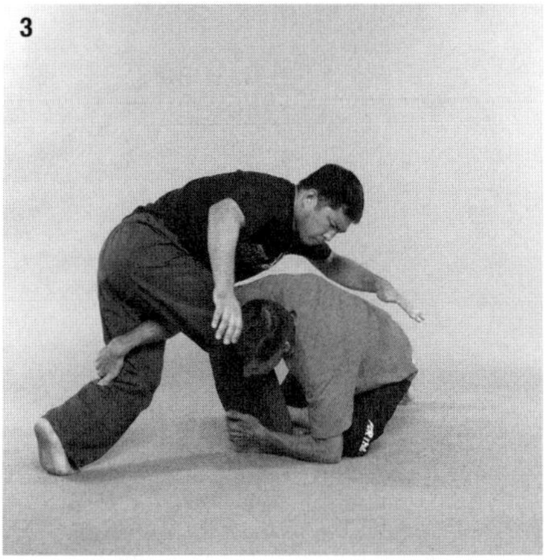

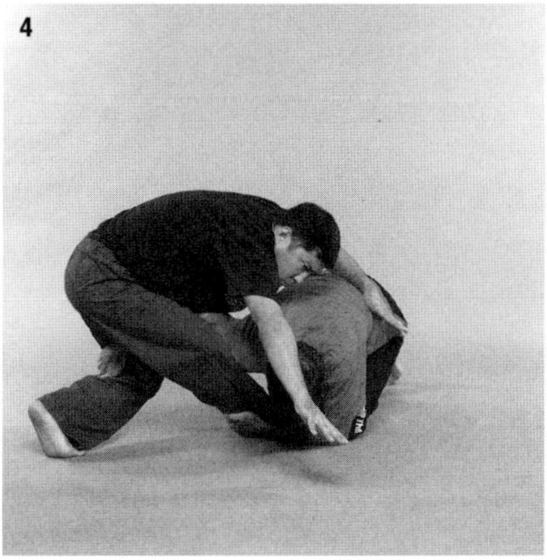

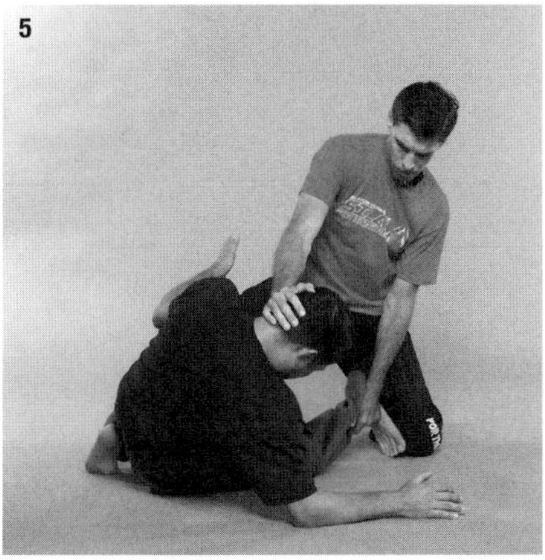

From the low position, Burton Richardson attempts the knee-pull takedown against attacker Scott Ishihara (1). But Ishihara counters by cross-stepping to catch his balance (2). With one hand, Richardson maintains the hold on Ishihara's lead foot and weaves his top hand behind Ishihara's rear knee (3). Richardson pulls to block Ishihara's rear knee as he drives his shoulder into the lead knee (4). He finishes the takedown and brings his torso up into an upright posture to take the top position from which he can strike or escape (5).

Elbow Compression to Outside Foot Sweep

1

2

3

4

As Burton Richardson drives in with a side lever for an elbow-compression takedown (1), adversary Scott Ishihara is able to slide away and make space to counter (2). Richardson slides his lead hand back to grab Ishihara's shoulder (3-4). He's now able to pull Ishihara's body at the proper angle to apply an outside foot sweep and take him down (5-6).

CHAPTER SEVEN

CLINCH POSITIONS

Silat instructors often move in deep while striking and quickly transition to a takedown. But they also perform many moves in the range that martial artists today refer to as the clinch. This is the range at which you can physically grab the attacker and he can grab you.

If you charge in to take an aggressor down but you can't apply the throw, you are in the clinch. It is imperative that you don't just revert to trading blows but instead grip in a way that it is difficult for the attacker to strike or move you while maximizing your ability to strike, off-balance and throw the attacker. If you want to optimize your fighting ability, you must understand the different positions in the clinch, prioritize them in terms of functionality for self-defense, and train these positions so you can dominate the fight in close quarters.

The average attacker can throw a damaging punch from boxing range but usually doesn't have much more than a head lock in the clinch. This gives you a huge advantage if you are well-versed in close quarters with functional, street-specific skills. Blending Southeast Asian methods with a mixed-martial arts clinch yields tremendous results. And keep in mind that sparring in the clinch is also great fun!

As on the ground, if you don't understand the clinch and end up against someone who does, you are going to be dominated. If you find yourself sparring in the clinch with someone proficient in silat and even Filipino martial arts who has a lot of moves but does not spar in the clinch, you may discover that the opponent does not understand the structure and will leave openings. You will be able to take his back over and over again. Blending silat training with a strong MMA clinch approach is a huge advantage, allowing for defense, the application of street-specific attacks and transitions taken from wrestling and jiu-jitsu training.

This chapter demonstrates the major clinch positions used in functional silat. There are many variations of each, but these basics have proved themselves very useful in sparring for MMA fighters and silat students.

To be your best, you also should work in positions and tactics from wrestling. They fit very well into the silat matrix and give you more options.

Please note that in many of the positions, silat practitioners will grab the skin, muscle or nerves to further inflict pain and secure a better grip on the attacker. In sport training, practitioners make it a point to not pinch or gouge each other because it becomes irritating. But in silat, it is encouraged! Just be gentle when sparring.

Understanding, practicing and sparring in the clinch is essential if you want your silat to be effective in the modern MMA era. Regardless of your particular style, be sure that clinch sparring is a normal portion of your training so that you can discover which techniques work best for you, then hone them to a fine edge.

DOUBLE-BICEPS GRAB

The double-biceps grab is very simple, works against much larger and stronger opponents, and checks each arm so you can monitor whether the aggressor is about to draw a weapon. A problem with some sport clinch positions is that they are meant to be used against someone in the same weight class. (A simple move like the neck clinch, for example, can be difficult against someone much taller.) In silat, it is assumed that the attacker is bigger and stronger, so the priorities change.

Unlike the neck clinch in which you secure the body, the double-biceps grab has you hanging off the attacker's arms. This gives you a lot more leverage because your grip is farther from your adversary's core. You are using almost your entire bodyweight on the arms, near the elbows.

Grab both biceps with your hands, using your thumb and fingers to grip into the muscles. The thumb looks for the nerve that runs inside the arm just below the biceps. Be in a forward-lever position, with your head on the attacker's upper chest. This keeps you clear of head butts, but you can rear back at any time and deliver one of your own. As soon as you secure the position, fire knees or snap kicks to the groin. Maintain forward pressure to keep the assailant from moving back out of range. As he works to free his arms, you can transition to his back, to throws, to strikes or switch to another clinch position.

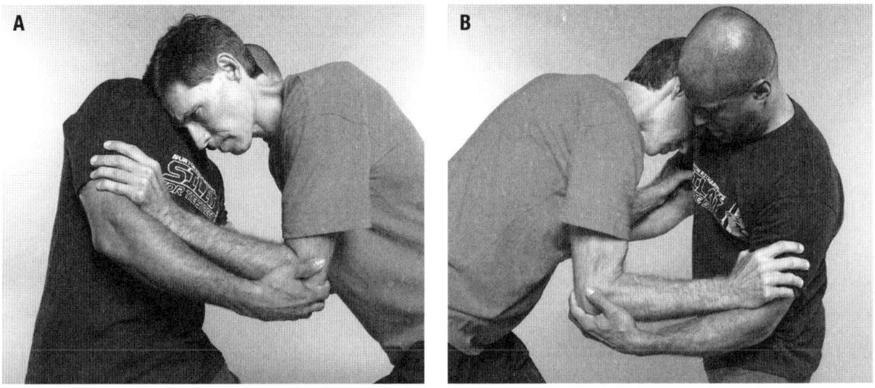

Double-biceps grab viewed from both sides (A-B)

1

2

3

4

5

6

Israel Cruz swings (1). Burton Richardson uses the dive entry with a forearm smash to the face (2). He drops his hands down for the double-biceps grab (3). Since he is close, Richardson throws knees to the groin (4). Cruz backs his hips away from the knee strikes (5). Richardson fires a front kick to the groin (6).

SNAKE

The snake is a natural way to control an attacker's arm. Your arm slithers over and around the attacker's upper arm and constricts to secure control. Once you have the snake, the attacker's arm is well-trapped.

Be sure that your arm is down near his elbow. This maximizes your leverage against him by putting weight farther from his core. The higher you go on his arm toward his shoulder, the stronger he is, and he can possibly use the position for his own underhook, which gives him control of your body.

If your left arm does the snake, engage your biceps to create constriction on his arm. Drop your weight so he is working hard to maintain his posture. Your free hand can strike, but that leaves his other hand free to strike you. You may overwhelm him with strikes to the eyes, throat or groin with your free hand, but a safe tactic is to use your open hand to control his free hand. Grasp the wrist or biceps to keep him from hitting you and to monitor the drawing of a weapon. Throw knees and kicks to the groin, head butts and/or go for a takedown.

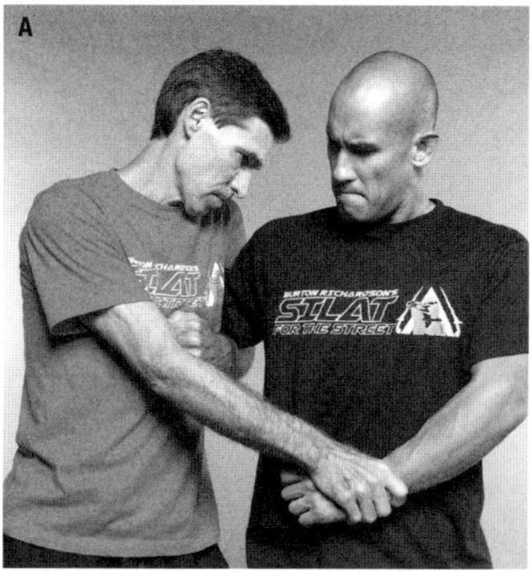

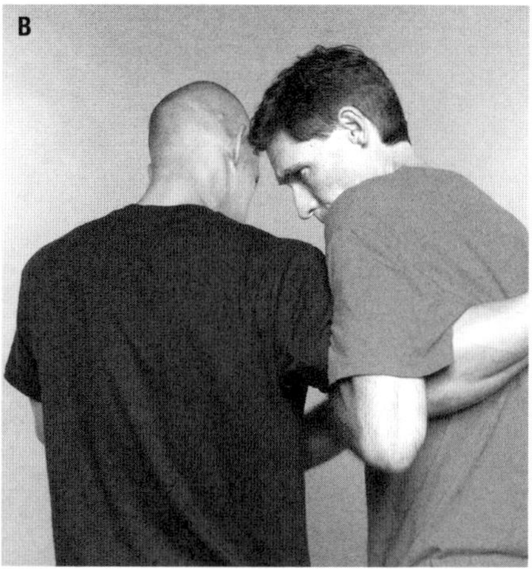

Snake viewed from front and back (A-B)

When Jarlo Ilano launches a rear hook, Burton Richardson uses a high cover to block (1). He enters deep with a side lever (2). Richardson wraps his blocking arm over Ilano's right for the snake (3). He traps the far arm to keep it from firing. Head butts are often possible from the snake position (4).

TRACHEA PINCH/THROAT GRAB

The trachea pinch and throat grab are simple moves in the clinch that work wonders. Grab someone's throat and all his attention goes there. It is also a great way to off-balance large opponents because it is a high lever point and it tends to put them up on their toes.

For the trachea pinch, grip around the trachea with your fingers and thumb. Drive upward as you pinch into the nerves that are behind and at the top of the trachea while driving with forward pressure.

The throat grab is similar to the trachea pinch, but you grip the entire throat instead of going specifically for the trachea. The advantage is that it takes less precision, is easier to apply under stress and the effect is very similar to the trachea pinch.

Grip around the throat as high as you can with the Y of your hand (the area between your thumb and index finger), pressing hard against the trachea. Drive diagonally upward to get the attacker on his tiptoes while using forward pressure to push the person backward.

In both moves, stay close to the attacker so you can maximize your leverage by using your leg and hip strength to drive upward.

You will usually want to use your free hand to check the nearest arm, but if the attacker has hair to grab, you also can reach behind and take hold of it. Throw knees and snap kicks to the groin, or look for a way to take the attacker down. Simple and effective!

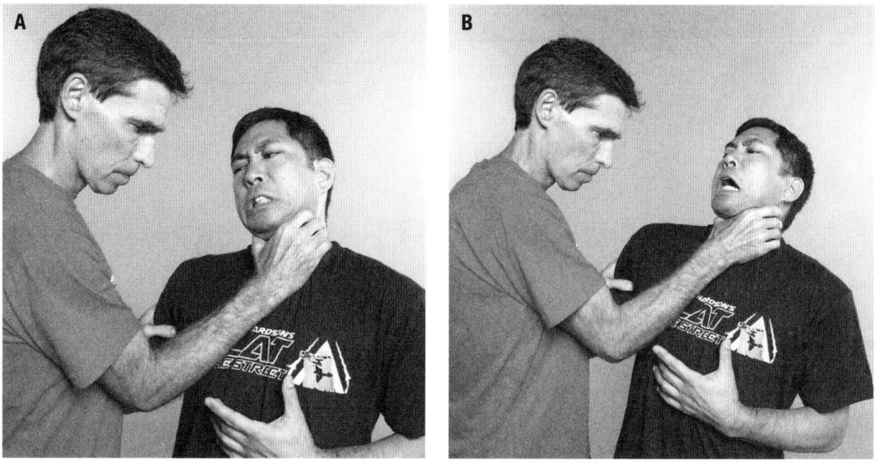

Trachea pinch (A) and throat grab (B)

1

2

3

4

When two people clash, they often end up in a neutral position in which they each have an arm under one of the other's (1). This is a great place from which to transition to the dominant throat-grab position. Burton Richardson pulls out his underhooked arm and grabs Scott Ishihara's throat (2-3). Richardson uses forward pressure to drive into the attacker (4). There are many striking and throwing options from here, such as the throat-grab takedown.

SUPPORTED TRACHEA PINCH/THROAT GRAB

When you grab someone's throat, they will usually use both hands to pull your hand away. It is a natural reaction. To make that very difficult, use the other arm to support the trachea pinch or throat grab.

If you pinch or grab with the right hand, use your left to snake the assailant's right arm. Your left hand will go palm up and grab underneath the forearm of your pinching arm. Push up with the supporting left hand to counter the downward pull of the attacker. This gives you more time to throw knees and kicks to the groin as the attacker tries to remove your grip.

You will sometimes see the supported throat grab with the supporting arm gripping over the top of the wrist. This does nothing to counter the attacker's downward pull.

The supported trachea pinch/throat grab is a highly effective move, one of the primary clinch positions and one that you should master.

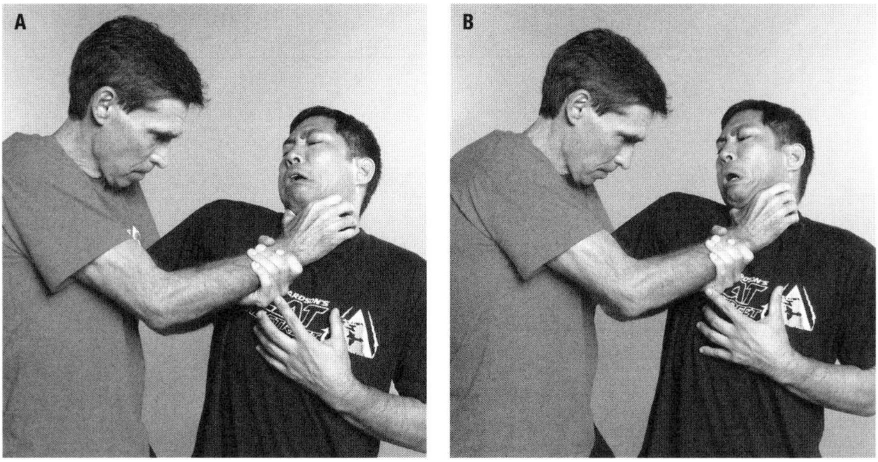

Supported trachea pinch (A) and supported throat grab (B)

Scott Ishihara swings a stick at Burton Richardson's head (1). Richardson uses the dive entry to get inside the blow (2). He snakes the stick arm (3), then transitions to the supported throat-grab position (4-5).

SINGLE NECK CLINCH

This is a simple, instinctive and highly functional position. *Tatang* Antonio Ilustrisimo used this position a great deal. Simply grab the back of the neck to control the attacker and start striking. Be sure to dig the ends of your fingers into the assailant's neck for better grip and to cause a distraction. Keep your elbow down so your forearm is pressed against the aggressor's clavicle to make tackling you difficult.

You can check the other arm and throw knees and kicks, or you can go directly to striking or gouging the eyes with your free hand. Counterattack ferociously to upset the mental and physical balance of the aggressor.

Single neck clinch

Israel Cruz fires an elbow (1). Burton Richardson drives with a side lever and grabs the back of Cruz's neck to block the elbow and puts himself into the single neck-clinch position (2). In a very serious situation, Richardson can step back and load up a knuckle uppercut to the throat (3-4).

THAI NECK CLINCH

This is a position that muay Thai fighters have cultivated to a very high level. In many silat techniques, the fighter grabs the neck or back of the head with both hands before throwing knees and kicks. The Thai-style neck clinch is precise because of its emphasis on head control while breaking the posture of the adversary.

Cup one of your hands behind the upper portion of the attacker's head. Use your elbows on the chest like a fulcrum to pull the attacker's head down while keeping your forearms tight around the neck to prevent the attacker from ducking out of the clinch.

Jerk the assailant's head down and twist it to the side. This keeps the attacker off-balance physically and mentally and makes striking and setting up throws much easier. Unlike students of the sport of muay Thai, silat practitioners usually strike to the groin unless the assailant protects himself. Knee strikes to the solar plexus and ribs are always available, and if you get the attacker bent over, a straight knee to the chin or face often results in a knockout.

A great benefit of the neck clinch is that it is a very easy position to attain when under pressure. We are hard-wired to grab an aggressor's head, and the neck clinch is an easy way to keep your fighting in line with your instinctual response when under the stress of a surprise attack.

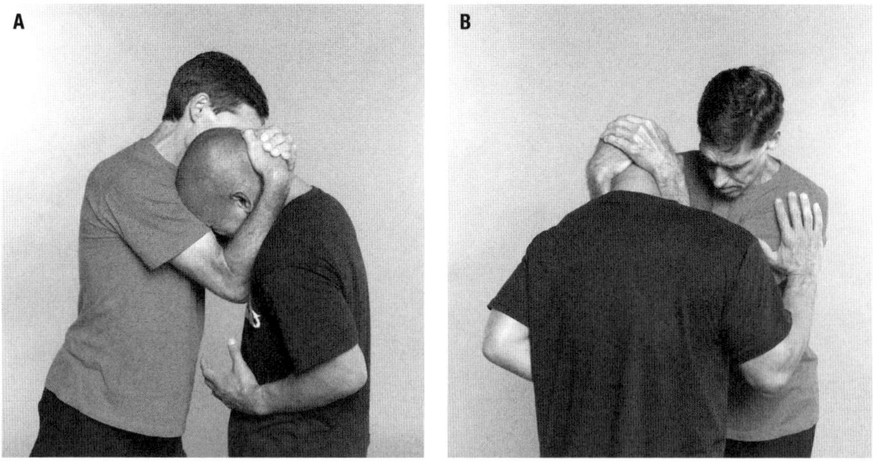

Thai neck clinch, two views (A-B)

From a kickboxing stance, Burton Richardson throws a flying knee at Jarlo Ilano (1-2). If it doesn't land, it will almost always get an adversary's hands down, making it easy to secure the Thai neck clinch (3). From there, the snap kick to the groin is a great option, especially because those who train combat sports don't practice defending against it (4).

DOUBLE THROAT GRAB

This is a very simple and effective move that is often looked down on, but it works! Do the throat grab with one hand while the other hand goes behind the neck to keep the attacker from backing out of the position. Lift up diagonally to make the aggressor stand on his tiptoes and look up. From here, you can head-butt, throw knees, back sweep, head-tilt or just slam the attacker into a wall for control.

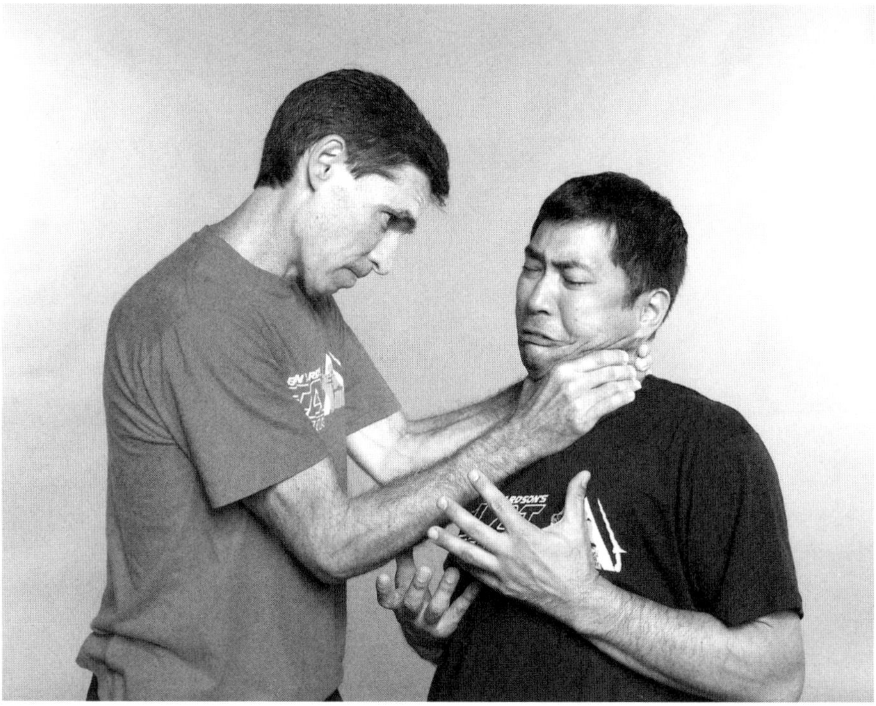

Double throat grab

Throat grabs are great for stopping someone who is trying to tackle you. Scott Ishihara changes levels to prepare to shoot in (1). As he does, Burton Richardson bends his knees into a forward lever for stability and catches Ishihara by the throat (2). Richardson grabs the back of the neck for the double throat grab (3). He drives Ishihara's head up and back (4), then pulls him into a devastating knee strike to the groin (5).

BEAR HUG

The peluk (bear hug) is a common position in village silat tournaments. Often, when the fighters get very close, one will go for a bear hug to control the opponent and immediately try for a takedown, often lifting and slamming. It is an important position to know and to be able to counter.

Get both your arms under those of the attacker. If you hold very high, you will severely limit the attacker's arm motion and you can transition to a trip. If you grip low on the torso, you can lift and throw, but the person might be able to use his hands in your face or eyes to push you away.

The key is posture so you don't end up bent over and lifting with your lower back. Maintain good posture as you grasp the assailant's body and use forward pressure with your legs to control the attack and set up a takedown. Sparring with wrestlers who do this for a living will greatly enhance your bear-hug offense and defense.

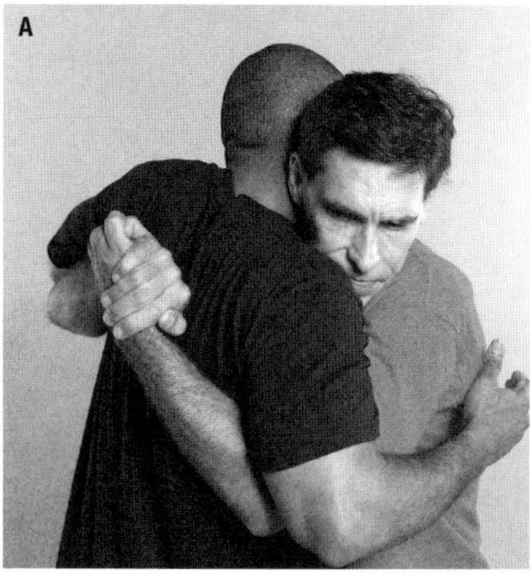

High bear hug (A) and low bear hug (B)

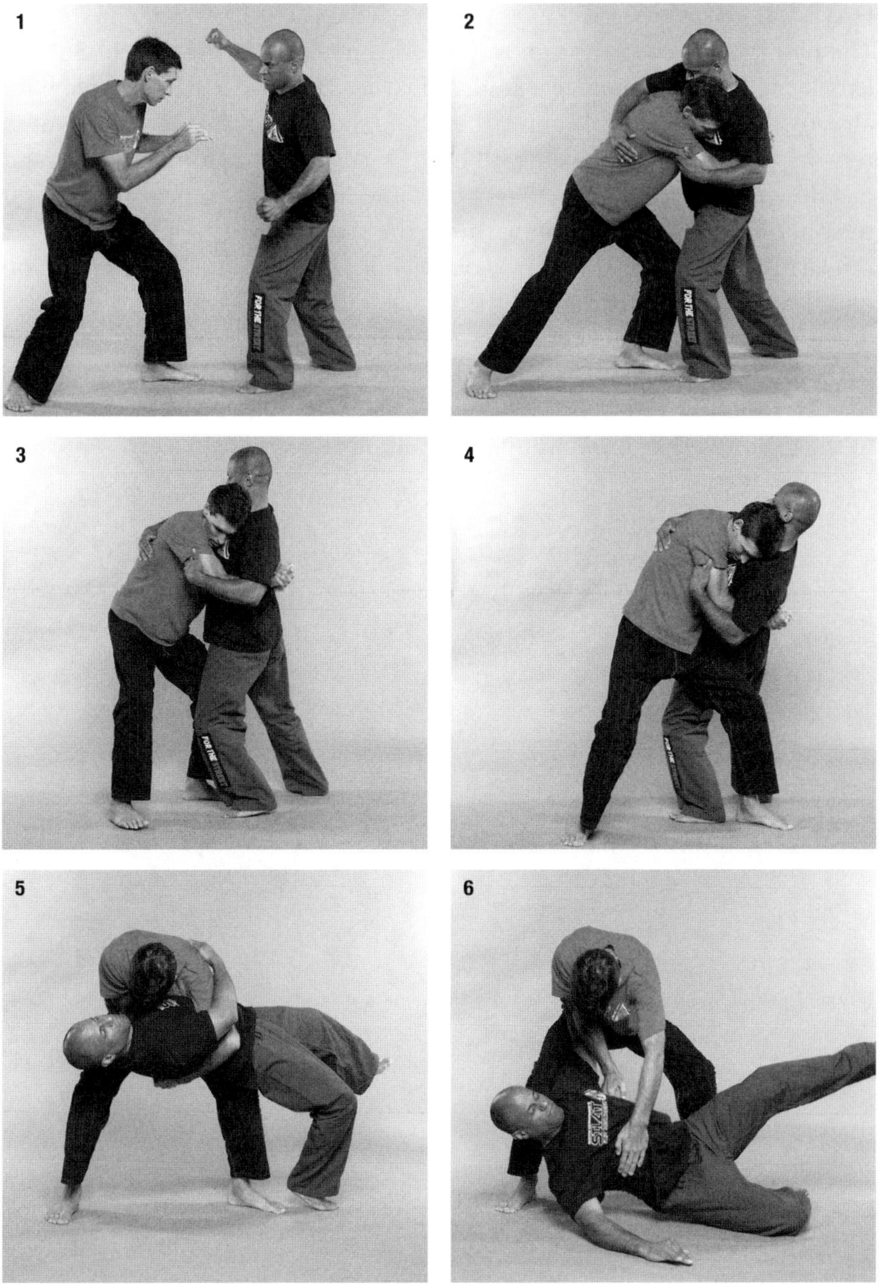

Israel Cruz takes a swing, and Burton Richardson ducks (1). He enters to the bear-hug position with a forward lever (2). Cruz stabilizes his base to avoid an immediate takedown (3). Richardson steps his left leg behind Cruz's left (4) and then turns hard to apply the outside back sweep (5). The result for Cruz is a hard fall (6).

HAIR GRAB

The hair grab is the safest, most powerful position in the clinch. So why isn't it the first clinch move a student learns? Because a lot of people have already countered it by keeping their hair short! Just as you don't want to rely on whether an opponent will have sturdy clothing for your grips and takedowns, you don't want to rely on someone having hair to grab. But if the opponent does have a mop, this is the go-to move.

Grip the hair on the upper, outer sides of the skull. This gives you handles with which to control the attacker. Step back and snap the head down so the attacker is bent over. Keep your arms almost fully extended to maintain your distance and limit the assailant's attack options. You can now kick to the groin, knee to the face, sweep a leg or just jerk the opponent to the ground. That is a dominant clinch position!

Hair grab

1

2

3

Anytime you are inside punching range, you can grab an attacker's hair and gain maximum control. Against Scott Ishihara's left swing, Burton Richardson uses the helmet to block the strike (1). He simply reaches out to execute the hair grab, pulling Ishihara forward and off-balance (2). The groin kick is the most efficient strike from here, and ripping the opponent to the ground is quite easy (3).

BENT ARM LOCK WITH CHIN GRAB

This is a position in which you can easily rip the assailant to the ground or crash the person's head into a solid object. It can be referred to as the "ramming position."

It's most efficient to get to this position from a wrestling underhook. Get the assailant bent over by firing a knee to the groin, by a sweep or by jerking the neck. Then grab the attacker's chin. Since you are facing the attacker directly, you will feel stuck and will only be able to twist the head a little. To alleviate the binding problem, let your underhooking hand slide down to the middle of the triceps so you can turn and face the person. Now apply the bent arm lock and pull the chin upward. The assailant is stuck. From here, knee the head, knee or kick the groin, ram the attacker into a barrier or execute a throw straight to the ground. Note that if the aggressor is sweaty, your chin grip can slip.

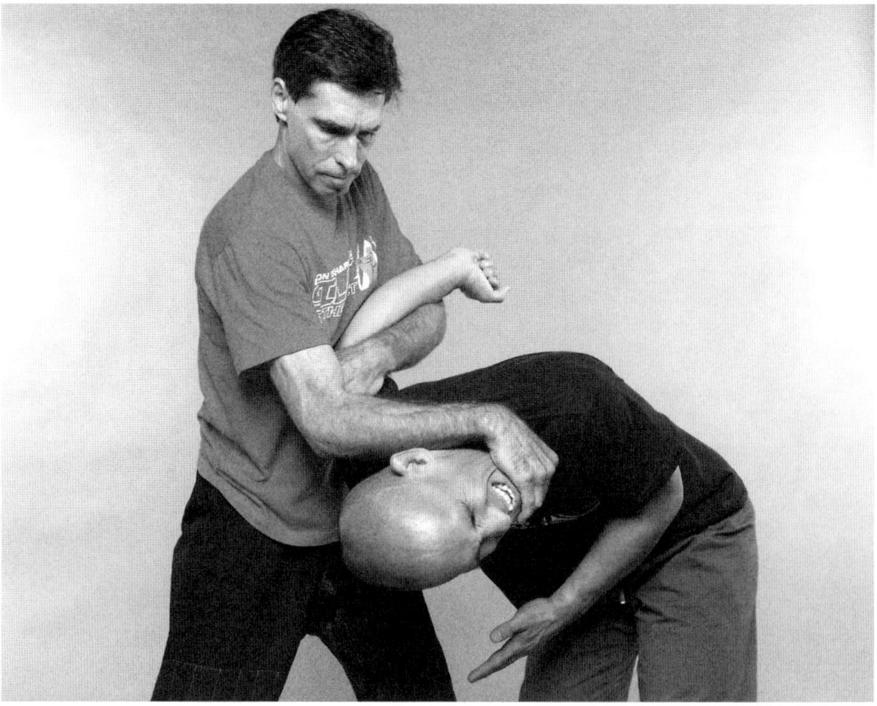

Bent arm lock with chin grab

1

2

3

4

5

Starting with an underhook, Burton Richardson attempts an inside back sweep (1). Jarlo Ilano is able to keep his base and tries to enter for a takedown (2). Richardson moves his hips away and captures Ilano's head by grabbing his chin (3). Richardson slides his underhooking hand down to the elbow while twisting Ilano's head and arrives in the bent-arm-lock-with-chin-grab position (4-5).

SILAT TWO ON ONE

This is a very common grabbing position in silat and in kali. Just know that you will only be able to keep this grip and angle momentarily on the attacker before he pulls out or turns to face you.

The silat two on one is often shown against a punch, but punches with violent intent travel too fast to be snatched out of the air. In reality, you would use the two on one against a push or a grab attempt, or you would create it in the clinch.

Take both hands from the outside of the attacker's arm and grab the triceps near the elbow with your palm facing up. The other hand will grasp the wrist either palm up or palm down, depending on your preference and anticipated follow-up. Use your fingers to dig into the biceps and nerves.

You have very little time, so attack immediately. A quick kick to the groin or other available targets works well, as does a head butt or knee if you are quite close to the attacker. You also can push the arm across the assailant's body to put you in position to tilt the head, slap the groin or move to the attacker's back.

An early addition to our MMA clinch game, this silat move has proved very useful against highly skilled fighters. Many law-enforcement officers now use the position to control suspects.

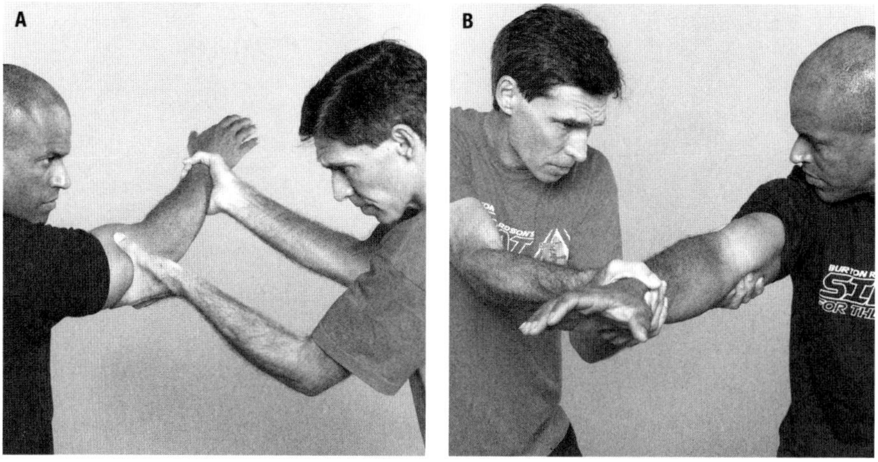

Silat two on one, viewed from both sides (A-B)

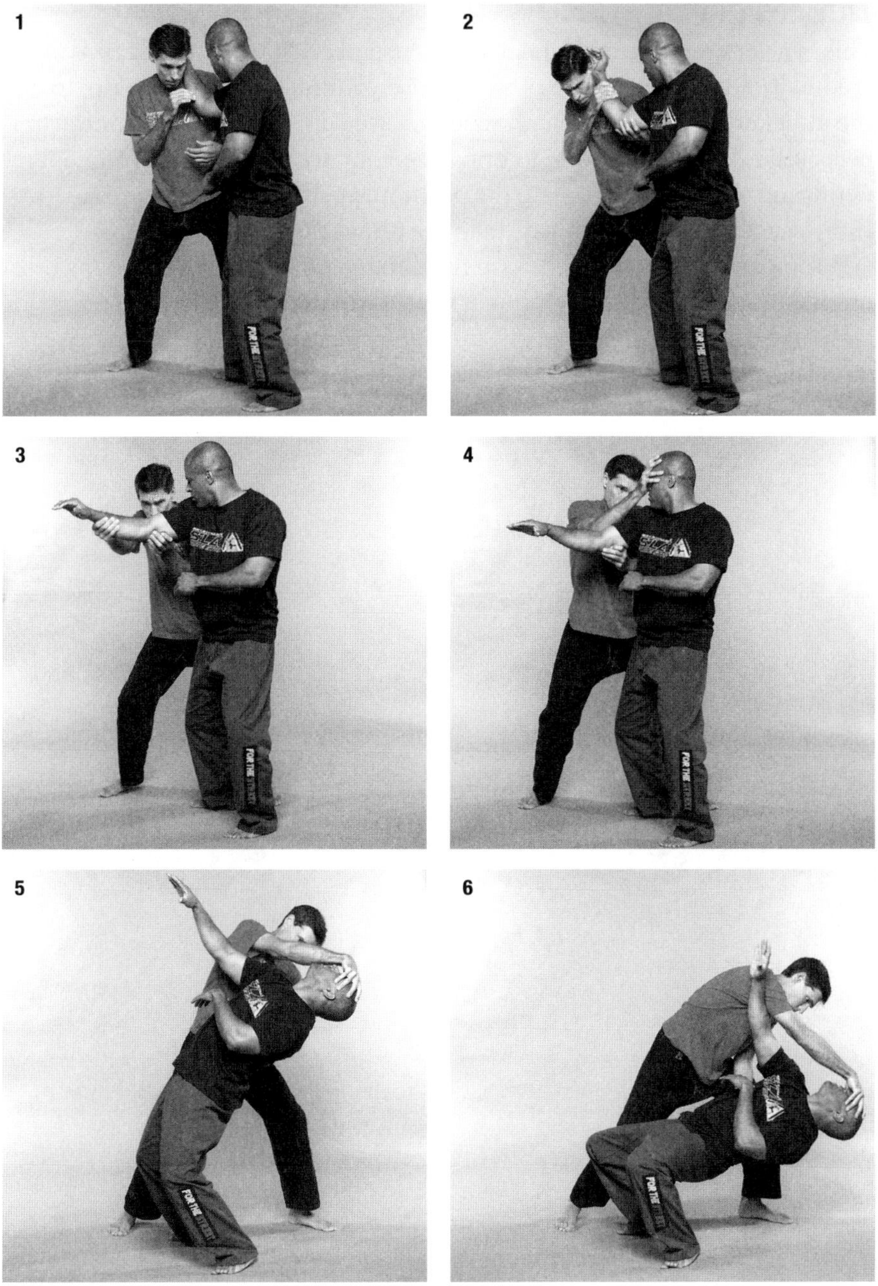

Israel Cruz has a single neck clinch on Burton Richardson (1). Richardson turns his body and grabs at the wrist and triceps to remove the hold (2). As Richardson pushes the arm away, Cruz stiffens up and pushes back (3). Richardson slams his right hand into Cruz's upper face (4), then he transitions into the head-tilt takedown (5-6).

TRICEPS CUP

This is a very temporary but extremely useful position. It could be considered half of the two-on-one position. Use your lead hand, palm up, to cup the attacker's triceps. Turn and face the attacker's arm so that your arm is perpendicular to your body to optimize your structure. For a momentary tie-up and to elicit a reaction to the position, push the assailant's arm across. If the reaction is to turn away, take the attacker's back.

You can get to the triceps cup from many positions, but perhaps most often when grabbing the opponent's biceps and he tries to pummel inside your arm. Slide your hand to the outside and get the triceps cup, make the attacker uncomfortable, then take advantage of the reaction.

Triceps cup

1

2

3

4

5

Burton Richardson executes the double-biceps grab (1). Israel Cruz swims his right hand from underneath, looking for the preferable inside spot (2). Richardson reads this reaction, rotates his left hand to Cruz's right triceps and pushes to get the triceps cup (3-4). Richardson immediately uses his positional advantage to deliver a palm strike to the groin (5). This is a simple way to pick up the triceps-cup position against someone trained in grappling.

DOUBLE-WRIST GRAB

Simply grab both the attacker's wrists. Once you have both wrists, extend your arms down and slightly away from your body. Lean on the opponent's arms like you are doing a dip on parallel bars. This gives you the leverage advantage, and it will take the opponent a little longer to get free from your grip. The attacker is going to find a way out of the move in a hurry, so counterattack right away with head butts or by throwing kicks to the groin.

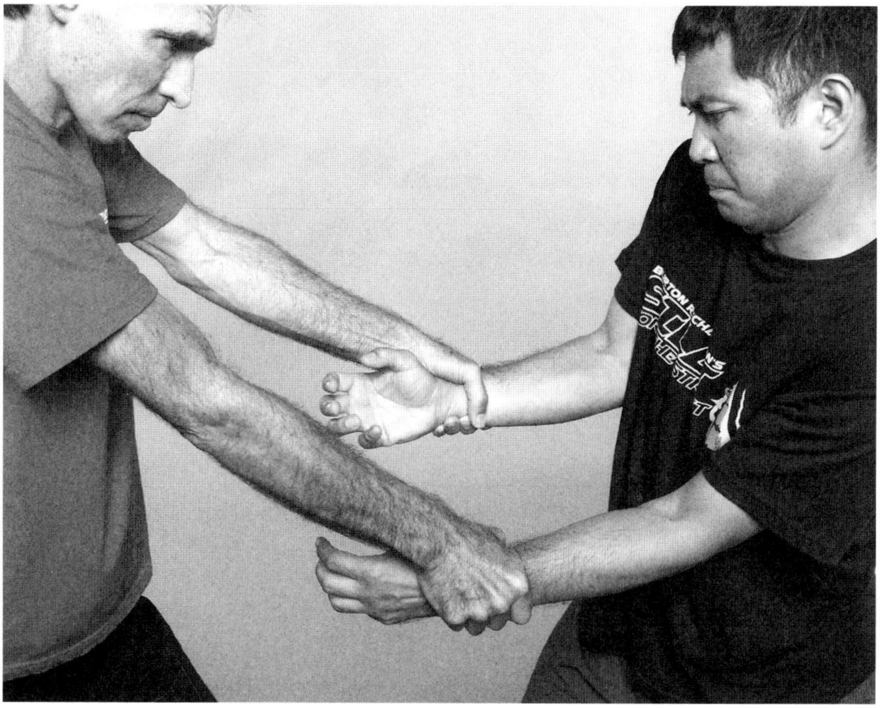

Double-wrist grab

Burton Richardson deals with Scott Ishihara's aggression from a disguised ready position (1). Richardson counters the two-hand shove by using the flower block from inside (2). He rotates his hands outward to achieve the double-wrist grab (3). It is difficult to retain this position for long, so Richardson immediately fires a powerful kick to the groin (4).

CHAPTER EIGHT

GROUND FIGHTING

Silat is a war art, so, historically, grappling was done out of necessity if a warrior slipped or was taken to the ground or to capture a valuable enemy to hold for negotiations or ransom. Usually, fighting on the ground involved pulling a blade and finishing the downed opponent.

Today's different styles of silat delve into empty-handed, one-versus-one ground fighting to varying degrees. Many prefer the pukulan approach of just striking the opponent into submission. Others have a large repertoire of locks and holds. And many are somewhere in the middle with striking and a few grappling-specific techniques.

A problem that exists for many martial arts also appears in silat ground fighting — lack of training against a resisting opponent. When you just work with a compliant partner, you can create all kinds of positions without realizing that, in real life, those moves would be very difficult to apply, or worse, that you would be putting yourself in danger. But if you want to learn how to fight, you must practice fighting against someone who is fighting back — that also goes for the ground. If you want to learn how to grapple, you must practice grappling against someone who is grappling back — and preferably, against someone who is skillful in ground fighting, including strikes.

Functional-silat ground fighting is about finishing the fight as quickly as possible. You don't have time to patiently move from position to position because other attackers, who may be armed, are on the way. This is the assumption, so the primary attacker must be neutralized quickly. This is why as soon as the fight hits the ground, almost all silat systems prioritize striking, usually to the groin, eyes or head. If the opportunity presents itself, joint breaks are also used. Notice that submission locks are not a priority because the goal is not to have the attacker tap out. In the street, what happens after you make a violent assailant tap out to an arm lock? Are you going to let go of the lock and allow him to continue his assault? Of course not. So going for the tap is not an option in silat.

Joint manipulation is used to break a finger, wrist, arm or shoulder quickly before continuing with the overwhelming counterattack. Once the assailant is neutralized, you escape.

Although the silat fighter assumes that there is no time to patiently pursue locks, there are situations in which grappling can be applied very effectively for self-defense. This chapter explores some very functional silat-based ground fighting. You will either be working from a favorable top position or from an inferior bottom position.

Thoughts on Effective Grappling

I knew a lot of techniques on the ground when I first started Brazilian *jiu-jitsu,* but I could not apply any of them the first time I rolled with a small white belt who only had about six months of experience. I didn't have the sense of positioning required to hold my partner in place to apply any of my knowledge. After more than 20 years of consistent ground sparring, I am currently a two-stripe black belt in BJJ, so I know something about effective grappling. My advice to *silat* practitioners is to try out your grappling on someone with BJJ experience. It is true that you can't do eye gouges and groin strikes, but you will learn a great deal by training with experienced grapplers. If you are humble enough, you will do this in order to discover what you are doing well and where you need work. If you aren't willing to try this out, I suggest you do some introspection and find out what is holding you back from such a valuable experience.

I mention this because I often see silat practitioners demonstrating ground-fighting locks or flows that would never work against anyone with even a little grappling experience. It makes silat look bad to those who know how to fight on the ground, so they dismiss the entire art as useless. And that is a shame because silat has so much to offer. Keep it real for your sake and for the reputation of the art!

TOP POSITIONS

Squat and Strike From Top

This is a staple of silat ground fighting. As soon as you take the assailant down, you move to his head, squat and rain down punches. In the silat of old, this position also was used to thrust multiple times with a knife. Do that today against an empty-handed assailant and you are going to prison.

The squat-and-strike method is very safe because you don't actually engage the assailant on the ground. It is difficult for the attacker to grab or strike you, and since you are on your feet, you are highly mobile and can escape at any time. You just have to watch for a trained attacker rolling up to grab a single leg or rocking back and putting you in the guard.

You also can kick to the head or body, but be aware that a kick to the head of a downed attacker can get you in legal trouble. Only use the head stomp if you believe your life is still threatened, like when the downed attacker has a weapon.

The squat-and-strike method is extremely useful and aids in ensuring that you and the people you are protecting have ample time to make your escape.

Squat and strike from top

Kneel and Strike

This is the same concept as the squat and strike, but it allows you to use your elbows, as well, which is difficult from a squat. The downside is the proximity of your body and eyes to the aggressor — there's more opportunity for him to attack you.

You also can kneel on the opponent's body, but that leaves your groin open to attack if you haven't checked the aggressor's hands and puts you in grappling mode. This is why most silat practitioners prefer to kneel next to the downed assailant instead of on top of him like in jiu-jitsu or mixed martial arts. They want to avoid being grabbed and detained in case others are coming to join the fight.

Kneel and strike

BREAKS

Arm Break

Say you are in the squat position striking an assailant who rolls away and extends an arm in a desperate attempt to fend off your punches. You can move that arm and continue striking, or you can use the opportunity to injure it. Grab the assailant's arm at the wrist and pull down so that your shin is just above his elbow. Ballistically pull the arm back while thrusting your shin forward to hyperextend the elbow. This will render the attacker less dangerous, and you can then go back to striking.

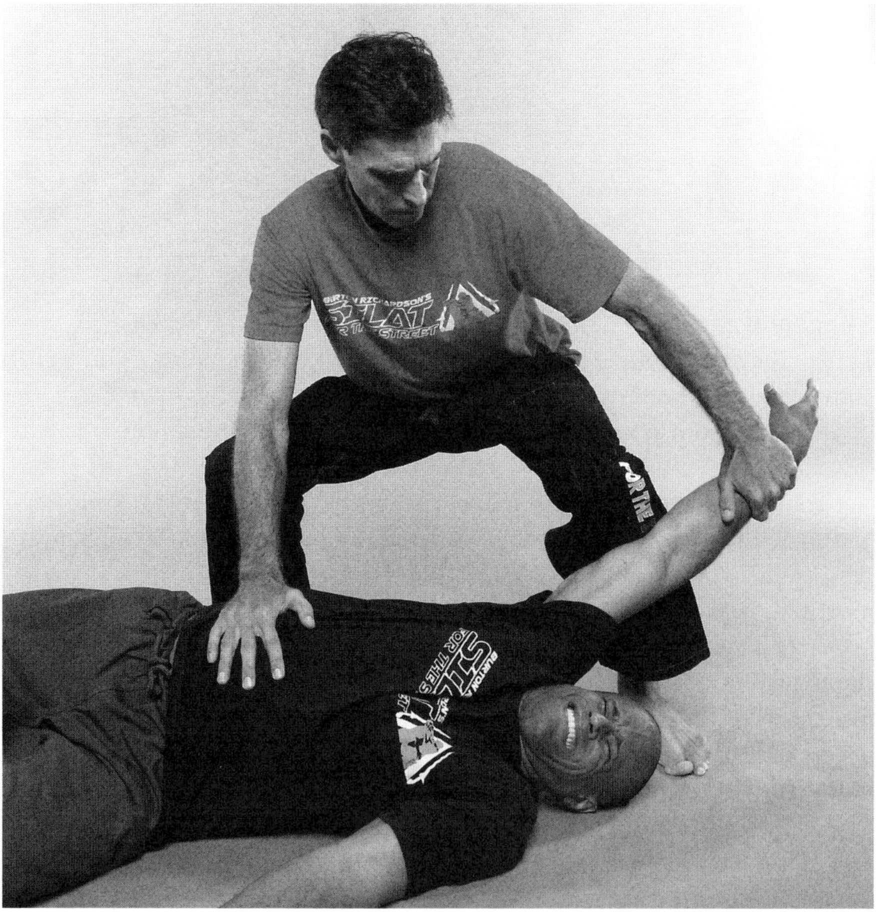

Arm break

Wrist Break

There are several positions in which to apply a wrist break, but here is an easy one. Again, if you are in the squat position, the attacker may roll on one side and cover his face, elbow pointing up. This gives you an opportunity for a wrist break.

Lower your squat to put one knee on the assailant's head and the other on his ribs. Grab the attacker's hand with both of yours. Secure the elbow against your chest and pull up ballistically to break the wrist. There are also twisting wrist breaks from this position. After the break, go back to hitting.

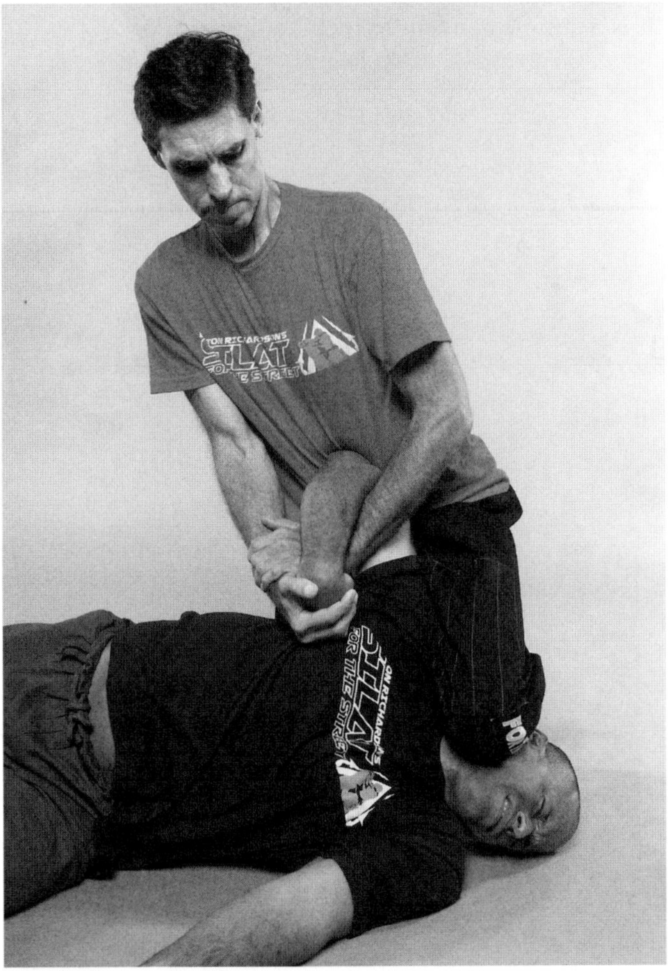

Wrist break

Finger Break

Here is a piece of advice from a Laotian silat man: "Any time you can grab a finger in a fight, break it!" It is difficult to grab fingers when you are in a striking fight, but in the clinch or on the ground, you have many opportunities.

It is easiest to break a finger if you first grab the attacker's hand and wrist. Slide down to grasp a finger. Using your wrist grab to keep the hand from moving, make a quick spiral movement against the joint to break it. You can then move to the next finger and do the same.

Like the gunslingers of the Old West, silat fighters like this because it makes it difficult for the assailant to later grasp a weapon and renew the attack. It is a simple concept to include in your flow.

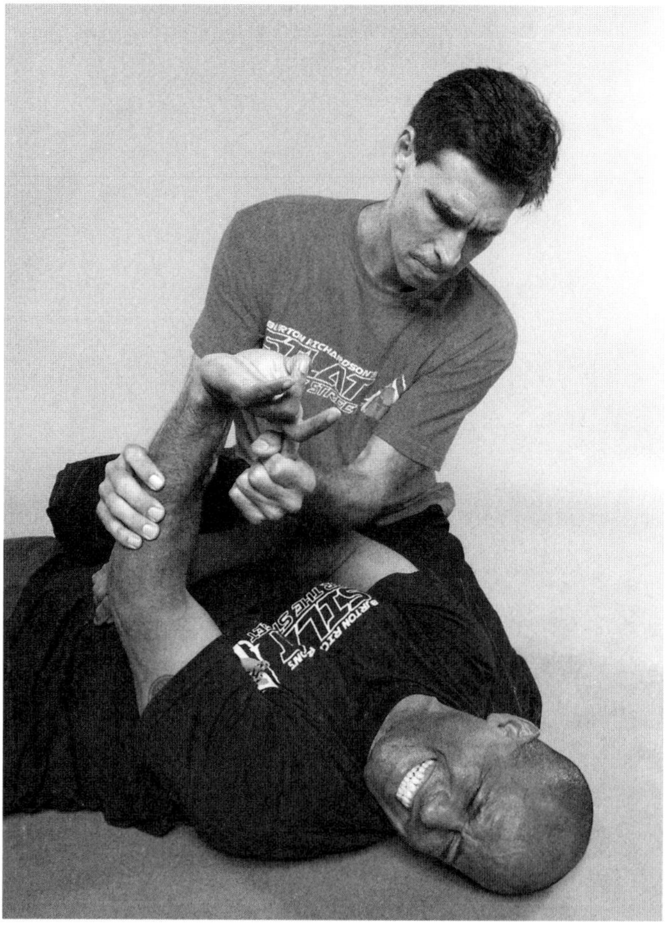

Finger break

Shoulder Break

If you have ever witnessed a shoulder tear, you know how devastating it is. People crumble from the pain. A shoulder break gives you a great advantage over an aggressor.

With the attacker on his side and covering his head, snake your left arm under his forearm while kneeling on his head. Reinforce your grip with your right hand, and turn explosively toward his head to torque his arm and dislocate his shoulder. If you don't block his waist with your leg, he will spin toward the direction of the break to alleviate the pressure. This needs to be done quickly and explosively. You can then let go and continue your counterattacking sequence.

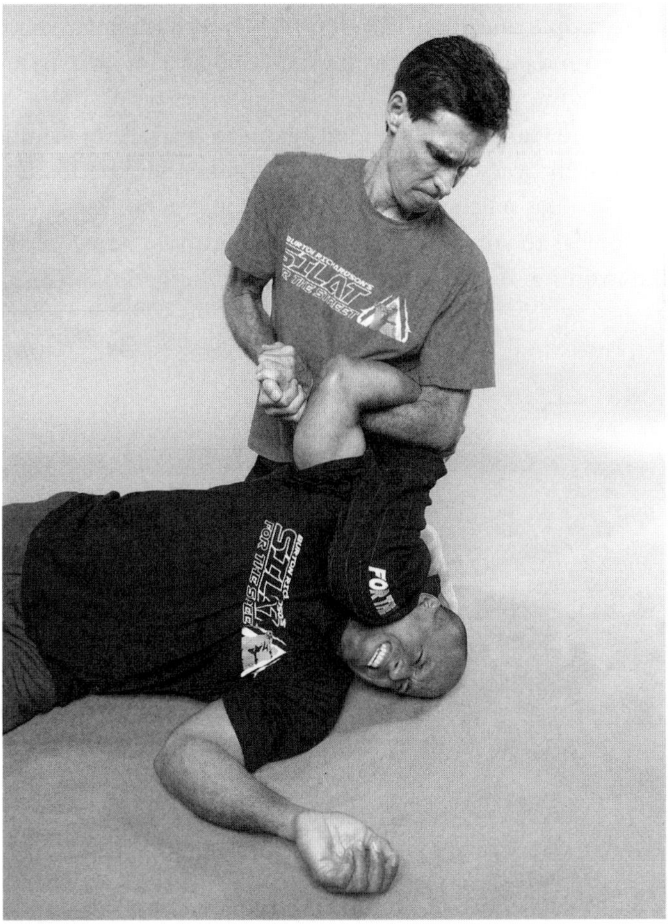

Shoulder break

SILAT IN THE GUARD

What happens when a silat expert ends up in the guard of a Brazilian jiu-jitsu expert? It all depends on how much functional-grappling experience the silat fighter has. The silat approach to being in the guard is to attack the groin or gouge the eyes of the adversary. This is absolutely valid, but fighting isn't just about knowing techniques or strategies. It is about having developed the attributes necessary to actually apply the moves against a skillful opponent. A good jiu-jitsu fighter is going to pull you off-balance, go for sweeps and fire submissions. If you are in the guard and unaccustomed to this barrage of attacks, you are going to end up swept or submitted. This is why it is so valuable to find some BJJ friends to grapple with. Work on your base and defense, then simulate the groin and eye strikes. If you know how to grapple and then add silat tactics into the mix, you will have a formidable ground game. Remember that it takes a lot of sparring time to be able to handle the guard of a decent grappler, so get in there, have fun, make mistakes and learn how to defend against a competent ground fighter.

Real fighters embrace anything that can make them better. If you want to truly have the silat on the ground, and not just pencak, take advantage of having grapplers in your midst. If you are a grappler, do yourself a favor and add silat training. It could save your life in a dangerous street situation.

Burton Richardson gouges Scott Ishihara's eyes from the guard. Notice that Richardson's elbows are down — not on Ishihara's chest — to avoid armbars and other submissions.

BOTTOM POSITIONS

Being on your back in a street attack is extremely dangerous. Your mobility is limited, the attacker can use gravity to strike down at you, and you are more vulnerable than ever to weapons and multiple attackers. If you are a good silat fighter and you end up on your back, you are going to attack while seeking to return to an upright position. Kicking to the groin or head, gouging the eyes, striking the groin or grabbing the throat are used to viciously attack the person on top. The intent is not just to distract but also to injure.

Experience in working to apply silat techniques against world champion grapplers will tell you that the tactics work as long as the adversary has not gotten to a position of superior control. Striking while keeping the opponent at your feet (in what BJJ calls the open guard) works very well. If the opponent gets to your side, you have just a few options and you need good grappling skills to apply them. If the opponent is in a vastly superior position of control, like mount or at the back, your street tactics are pretty much useless. Even if you do get a finger into the assailant's eye, the person is going to shrug it off and start giving back the same or worse. You need grappling expertise to escape during that split second of distraction that an eye strike or groin hit gives you. It is a very bad idea to rely on "foul" tactics to escape from a bad position without having functional-grappling skills to back them up.

If you are versed in the guard, there are many silat-based options available to you when you are on your back. Here are a few examples of mixing silat tactics with grappling when fighting from your back.

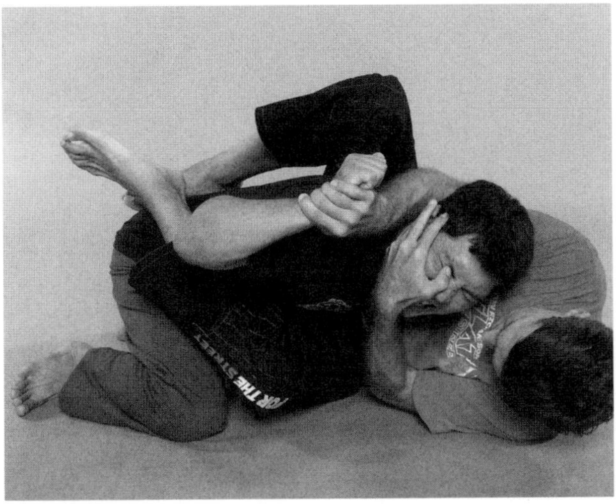

Example A

Burton Richardson has Scott Ishihara in his guard and keeps him close to avoid strikes. Richardson has Ishihara's left arm trapped with his body and reaches over Ishihara's neck to trap his right wrist. This allows Richardson to gouge the eye without any impediments.

1

2

3

Example B

Burton Richardson finds himself on the ground (1). He leans to the side to get out of the line of attack and puts his hands on the ground. He fires an unexpected kick with the shin to Scott Ishihara's neck (3).

1

2

3

Example C

Burton Richardson is on the ground in a harimau side-sitting position, hands out to block any punches from Scott Ishihara (1). Richardson unexpectedly springs up and forward to trap one arm (2). He ducks to the side to deliver an explosive open-hand strike to the groin (3).

1

2

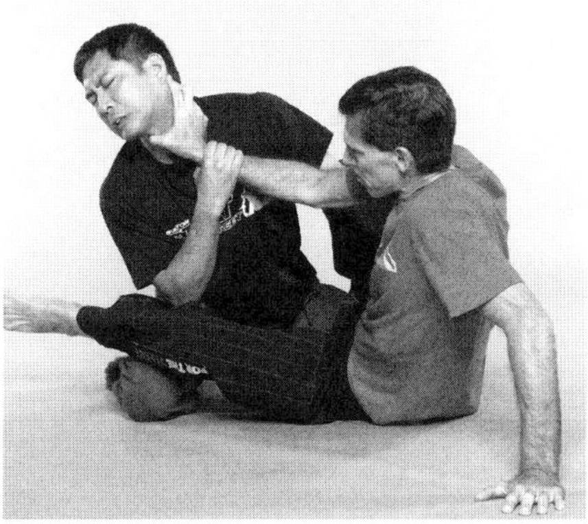

3

4

Example D

From his guard, Burton Richardson grabs Scott Ishihara's biceps with his left hand, to hinder striking, and Ishihara's throat with his right (1). While Ishihara is occupied pulling the hand off his throat, Richardson puts his left hand on the ground behind him (2). This allows Richardson to get to his knees and take the top position (3-4). This is a great move to get off the bottom. You can use this in sparring if your partners are street-minded and don't mind you grabbing the throat.

Grappling for Self-Defense

In modern culture, there are situations in which you may choose to grapple in self-defense. There are thousands of videos on the Internet showing street altercations involving prolonged ground fighting between two people without anyone else interfering. I call situations in which you can fight on the ground without an attacker's accomplice jumping in and booting you in the teeth "safe to grapple" scenarios. In some instances, there are onlookers but no one who wants to get involved; in others, a crowd gathers around to watch and acts as a referee imposing "fair fight rules"; and other instances might occur in an enclosed area like a home or office where it is just you and the intruder.

Because there are times when superior grappling skills work to your advantage, I highly suggest that you supplement your *silat* ground-fighting training with other forms of grappling. If you want to get really good at one-on-one grappling, do yourself a favor and cross-train. No system is perfect, so it is wise to take the best from Brazilian *jiu-jitsu,* wrestling, *sambo,* judo, mixed-martial arts grappling or any other grappling system. Learn different approaches and then mix in your silat tactics for a devastating combination. Potentially tens of thousands of willing training partners can help you improve by giving you skilled resistance in a safe environment. Take advantage of it. For a highly organized, functional, street-specific approach to ground fighting, check out my BJJ for the Street program.

Anyone interested in being truly skillful on the ground, regardless of style, would be wise to invest time training with seasoned grappling practitioners, especially with striking included. In addition, safely add strikes to the groin, throat grabs, simulated eye gouges and weapons to the mix, like in the BJJ for the Street program. It is more realistic and a lot more fun!

CHAPTER NINE

SARONG TACTICS

Sarong techniques are popular among many silat practitioners, but they often tend to skip over the simple, basic techniques and lean very heavily toward fantasy pencak. Most of the popular sarong moves rely on heavily choreographed sequences that require a trained, cooperative partner to feed you just right. These are techniques in which a partner throws a jab and cross, slowly of course, then stands there allowing his arms to be entangled before being strangled by the sarong. Just put the gloves on and try it out with some real resistance and see what happens.

Please don't forget the functional-sarong techniques, which tend to get lost because of all the emphasis on the flash and fantasy. Here are a few very effective sarong techniques that also can be used with a jacket or towel in Western culture.

Flashy? No. Effective in a street fight? Yes!

When doing sarong techniques, please know the difference between those that are done for the pencak performance art and those that are done for silat. If you have doubts as to which category your technique belongs in, just ask your partner to fight back and you will soon find out.

The Whip

One sarong technique Inosanto taught was to take the cloth and whip it at the eyes of the attacker, much like snapping someone with a towel. The end of the "whip" can be a distraction, or it can cause damage if you hit the eyes. Another move he demonstrated was a technique of some Southeast Asian stylists who would make a knot in one corner of the sarong or even tie in a few coins or pebbles for greater impact.

You can do the same with a jacket or towel. Whip the jacket out at the attacker to keep him away or distract him to set up an escape or counterattack. It's intuitive and very functional.

With Jarlo Ilano threatening (1), Burton Richardson readies the sarong (2). A towel, jacket, sweater, etc., also can be used. He whips it out, striking Ilano in the eye (3-4).

Put a Rock in It

Another sarong technique comes from a silat instructor from Bali. He suggests grabbing a fist-size rock, putting it in the sarong and swinging it around your head to hit the attackers, the assumption being that there is more than one assailant involved. The fast swinging is designed to keep them at a distance. It is another very simple, intuitive and highly effective method of using a sarong. With a jacket, you can put the rock in a pocket, zip it up and get swinging.

1

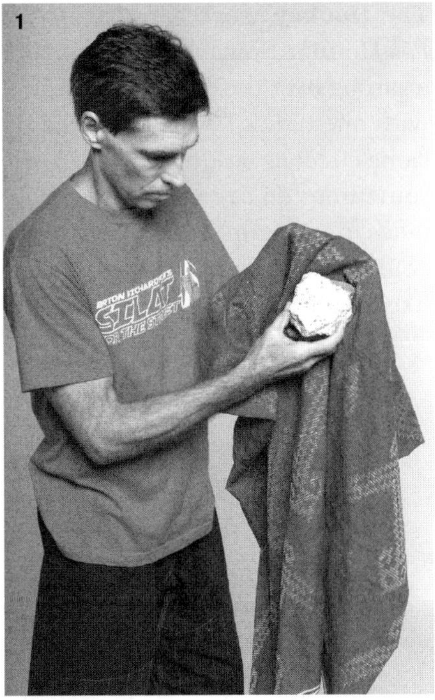

2

Place a rock or other solid object in the sarong (1), and swing the cloth (or jacket, towel, etc.) at high velocity toward the target (2).

The Hockey Move

Pak Herman Suwanda recommends the following sarong technique: Throw a sarong over the opponent's head to blind him and then hold the garment with one hand. It was given the name "hockey move" because it has the same effect as pulling the attacker's shirt over the head like hockey players sometimes do to each other on the ice. In a street situation, in the time it takes for the attacker to remove the sarong (or jacket) from his head, you could deliver several strikes or take the person down. If you have something like a sarong, jacket or towel, you can use the hockey move.

3

4

5

6

Jarlo Ilano threatens (1). As Ilano comes in to shove his would-be victim, Burton Richardson raises his arms with the sarong to deflect the attack (2). He covers Ilano's head with the cloth (3). He quickly brings the bottom edges of the cloth together while angling to the side to avoid Ilano's forward pressure (4). Richardson secures the sarong in place with one hand (5). With Ilano controlled and blinded, strikes or takedowns come easy for Richardson (6).

POSTSCRIPT

A CHALLENGE FROM BURTON RICHARDSON

I have a primary responsibility as an instructor to prepare my students and myself to be as fight-ready as possible. If I pass up a method that can help them be better prepared to defend themselves and their loved ones simply because it is from outside my system, then I am negligent as a teacher. As the Southeast Asian Burmese *bando* motto goes, "As no one nation has a monopoly on sunlight, no one system of thought can claim a monopoly on truth."

We can all learn and improve for the rest of our lives if we humble ourselves and admit that we don't know everything or have all the answers. This is especially true when we become instructors in a particular system. It is easiest to stay within the safe confines of our particular style where we are the experts and are revered for our knowledge. But that leads away from truth and toward stagnation. As one of my favorite quotes maintains, "A ship in harbor is safe, but that is not what ships are for."

Regardless of your particular style, I want to make sure that you can really use your *silat,* especially in a street fight against a trained combat athlete. I therefore again highly encourage you to use your silat knowledge in the realm of MMA-based training methods. Many "street" systems have a prejudice against combat sports, but there is much to learn from their constant preparation for actual fighting. Safe sparring in all the ranges? Yes. Hitting equipment? Of course. *(Muay Thai* is a silat derivative, and its development of the Thai pads was very important in that respect.) Physical conditioning? Absolutely. (Some silat methods already emphasize body toughening and stamina/strength building, but if yours doesn't, add that in.)

If you are an instructor, be sure to make each training session as enjoyable as possible for yourself and your students while keeping it safe and functional. People who are having fun train longer and more often. That is a recipe for success!

If you have questions for me or if you have a suggestion that can make my approach even better, please contact me. We are on this path together, and I am here to help.

Enjoy your *pencak* and enjoy your functional-silat training!